Demographic Transition Theory
Reinterpreted

Demographic Transition Theory Reinterpreted

An Application to Recent
Natality Trends in
Latin America

Steven E. Beaver
Stanford Research Institute
and
The Center for Policy Research

Lexington Books
D.C. Heath and Company
Lexington, Massachusetts
Toronto   London

Library of Congress Cataloging in Publication Data

Beaver, Steven E.
   Demographic transition theory reinterpreted.

   Bibliography: p.
   1. Demography. 2. Population. 3. Latin American—Population. I. Title.
HB901.B4   301.32'9'8   74-15544
ISBN 0-669-9626-5

Copyright © 1975 by D.C. Heath and Company.

Published simultaneously in Canada.

Printed in the United States of America.

International Standard Book Number: 0-669-96263-5

Library of Congress Catalog Card Number: 74-15544

To Cathy, Jennifer, and Joanna

Contents

List of Figures   xi

List of Tables   xiii

Acknowledgments   xvii

Introduction   xix

Chapter 1 **The Theory of the Demographic Transition:**
       Background and Logical Status 1

       Introduction 1
       The Malthusian Model 1
       Anomalous Empirical Trends 2
       The Theory of the Demographic Transition 4
       The Theory of the Demographic Transition
        as a Paradigm 10
       Specific Problems Currently Faced by the
        Theory 11

Chapter 2 **The Demographic Transition in Europe** 15

       Introduction 15
       Empirical Problems for the Theory 15
       The Timing of Natality Decline 17
       Empirical Support for the Theory 21
       Summary 22

Chapter 3 **The Demographic Transition in Non-European**
       Societies 25

       Introduction 25
       Japan 25
       The Developing World as a Whole 27
       Latin America 33

Chapter 4   A Respecification of the Theory   41

               Introduction   41
               Levels of Analysis   41
               The Fundamental Assumption   41
               Mortality   45
               Family Resources   48
               Cultural Background   49
               Excluded Variables   50
               Specific Hypotheses   53

Chapter 5   Methodology   61

               Introduction   61
               General Methodological Problems   61
               Means of Assessing Association of Variables
                   Other Than Regression Analysis   64
               Problems and Advantages of the Regression
                   Analysis   65
               Measurement   71

Chapter 6   Long-Term Sociodemographic Trends
                   (Hypotheses 1-4)   81

               Hypotheses 1a, 1b, and 1c   81
               Hypotheses 2a and 2b   93
               Hypothesis 3: Predicting the Occurrence of
                   Natality Decline   106
               Hypothesis 4   115
               Conclusions: Hypotheses 1-4   120

Chapter 7   Multivariate Analysis of Recent Natality
                   Trends (Hypotheses 5-9)   123

               Introduction   123
               Findings of the Simple Multilinear
                   Regression   124
               Problems and Refinements of the Regression
                   Analysis   133

Chapter 8 **Summary and Conclusions** 145

Previous Theory and Research 145
The Revised Causal Model 146
Findings 147
General Implications 151

Appendix 153

Bibliography 161

Index 173

About the Author 179

List of Figures

1-1   Causal Model of Demographic Transition
           Theory   10

3-1   Model of Income-Natality Relationship   33

3-2   The Relationship Between Overall
           Development and Natality in Latin
           America about 1960   35

4-1   Causal Diagram of the Influences on
           Natality   54

6-1   Gross Reproduction Rates During Natality
           Declines in Northwestern and Southern
           Europe and Latin America   91

List of Tables

2-1   Average Annual Declines in Crude Birth
Rate in European Countries   23

3-1   Zero-order Correlations Between Crude
Birth Rate and Eight Development
Indicators in Latin America   34

3-2   Annual Rates of Growth of Real Per Capita
Product and Real Total Product in
Percent   39

6-1 R^2 Values Resulting from Fitting
Various Functional Forms to Declines
in the Crude Birth Rate (CBR) of
European and Latin American Countries   82

6-2   Comparative Rates of Decline in CBR
Within Northwestern Europe   86

6-3   Comparative Rates of Decline in CBR in
Europe and Latin America   87

6-4   Comparison of Rates of Natality Decline
Based on CBR and GRR   92

6-5   Comparison of Rates of Increase in
Expectation of Life at Birth and Rates
of Natality Decline   96

6-6   Decadal Improvements in Mortality Measures   98

6-7   Rates of Development and Natality Decline   102

6-8   Change in Primary and Secondary School
Enrollment Per 10,000 Population and
Percentage of the Population Defined
as Urban, Countries with Natality
Decline   104

6-9   Mortality and Development: Comparison
             Countries Having Early Natality Declines
             with Others in Latin America   108

6-10   Mortality and Development: Comparison of
             Countries Having Recent Natality
             Declines with Other, High Natality
             Countries in Latin America   112

6-11   Countries of the Latin American Region
             by Racial Composition   117

6-12   Mean Residuals of the Regression Analysis
             of the Age-Sex Standardized Birth Rate
             According to Cultural Background
             (Openness-Exposure to Modernizing
             Influences) Indexed by Racial
             Composition   118

7-1   Results of the Regression Analysis   126

7-2   Natality Differences Implied by Partial
             Regression on Land Availability   131

7-3   Results of the Regression Analysis with
             Variables Monotonically Transformed to
             Obtain Greater Linearity   135

7-4   Results of the Regression Analysis with
             Lags Increased by Five Years   136

7-5   Results of the Regression Analysis with
             Past Natality Controlled   139

7-6   Observed Serial Correlations in Residuals   141

7-7   Observed Serial Correlations in Residuals
             After Being Purged of Assumed Linear
             Autocorrelation from a First-order
             Markov System   142

7-8   Extreme Residuals   143

A-1   Matrix of Zero-order Correlations   155

A-2   Residuals (Deviations) of the ASSBR
               Regressed on the Independent Variables   156

A-3   Residuals (Deviations) of the CBR Regressed
               on the Independent Variables   157

A-4   Recent Natality Declines in Latin America
               as Measured by the Crude Birth Rate   158

Acknowledgments

Much of the research on which this paper is based was carried out pursuant to Contract No. NIH-702189 with the National Institutes of Health, Department of Health, Education and Welfare, as part of a larger study at Stanford University on "Socioeconomic Factors in the Reduction on Natality in the Less Developed Areas," under the direction of Professor Dudley Kirk.

I would like to express the greatest possible thanks to Professor Dudley Kirk for his tireless work and helpful advice on this manuscript. He spent untold hours with me—advising, debating, arguing, and encouraging—in an effort to improve the quality of this monograph.

I would also like to thank professors Michael Hannan and John Meyer for their guidance and inspiration. They were especially instrumental in carrying out the more novel research of this study, reported in Chapter 7.

Introduction

The theory of the demographic transition is the predominant body of thought in social demography. A very large number of theoretical and empirical works have been directed toward questions raised by the ideas and assertions of the theory. Despite this, there is considerable disagreement as to the basic status of transition theory at this time. The following quotations give a good indication of the two major contrasting positions:

Demographic transitions rank among the most sweeping and best-documented historical trends of modern times. . . . All nations in the Modern Era which have moved from a traditional, agrarian-based economic system to a largely industrial, urbanized base have also moved from a condition of high mortality and fertility to low mortality and fertility [Stolnitz, 1964:30].

The theoretical, methodological, and empirical inadequacies associated with these hypothesized relationships render the [demographic transition] theory virtually useless. . . . The theory provides minimum interest to the social scientist concerned with the determinants and consequences of population transformations [Goldscheider, 1971:14].

There are good reasons for the existence of such conflicting opinions, but it is more important to attempt to solve the underlying theoretical and empirical problems. This research is an effort in that direction.

There are also practical considerations that justify a new attempt to interpret and apply transition theory. Since World War II the world, especially the developing world, has undergone an unprecedented population increase, popularly termed the "population explosion." This phenomenon could be viewed as a prediction of transition theory, and if the theory predicts the "explosion," it also predicts that it is a temporary condition that will be alleviated by a massive natality decline. Whether and how this will come about is of critical importance. If transition theory can or can be made to deal with this question, it is far more than an exercise in historical demography. It deals with the future fate of most of humanity. This book seeks to improve and test the applicability of transition theory concepts to the developing world by means of an analysis of the experience of Latin American countries.

Chapter 1 examines the origins and logical status of the theory of the demographic transition. This body of thought may be viewed as a typology, an empirical generalization, a sociodemographic theory, or a paradigm for sociodemographic research. Recognition of this multifaceted characteristic helps to clarify some of the misunderstandings about the theory. The present approach interprets the demographic transition as a sociodemographic theory which relates social structure to demographic variables. Specifically, it proposes to explain why a society undergoing socioeconomic development experiences mortality and natality decline in a certain manner. While the theory seeks to explain both natality and mortality trends, we will invariably treat natality as the primary dependent variable and will discuss mortality mainly as an independent variable.

Chapter 2 reviews some of the research that has dealt with the demographic transition in European nations. Although the theory was formulated with this experience in mind, it fails to explain some of the salient features of European natality trends. On the other hand, some researchers have pointed out empirical "anomalies" that are either beyond the scope of the theory or could be explained by the theory if additional assumptions about lag times and the nature of socioeconomic development were included. Some possible explanations for anomalous observations are considered; these usually involve ideas that are outside the scope of demographic transition theory but not contradictory to it.

Chapter 3 examines some of the research on the demographic transition in non-European countries. The experience of Japan seems to confirm the applicability of transition theory to the Third World, but broader cross-sectional findings relating to less-developed countries are puzzling. Results depend on the particular sample and procedures used, and investigators have not always accurately operationalized the theory. There do appear to be differences among the major cultural regions of the world. Furthermore, while measures of socioeconomic development are generally inversely correlated with natality, per capita income or product occasionally has a positive correlation when certain other variables are controlled. Finally, there are some instances in which, despite considerable socioeconomic development, natality has risen; the best documented of these are in Latin America.

In Chapter 4 a respecification of the theory is attempted. The most fundamental ideas of the theory are preserved, while adding some major refinements. The role of mortality change is examined in detail and found to be more complex than is suggested by transition theory. Allowance is also made for a "Malthusian" association between prosperity and higher birth rates, although this is assumed to be counteracted in the long run by urbanization and rising expectations. Finally, the role of cultural background in determining natality is considered. This idea is developed in terms of the predicted openness and/or exposure of various cultural types to modernizing influences.

Chapter 5 outlines the methodology to be used in testing the hypotheses, and considers certain problems in greater detail. There are two separate analyses. The first of these concerns long-term natality trends in the Latin American region and their major determinants; the second is focused on the post-World-War-II period in Latin America, and involves a more novel cross-sectional-longitudinal regression.

Chapter 6 reports findings relating to the first part of the analysis—the study of long-term trends. Considerable attention is directed to the quality and availability of natality data, in an attempt to determine natality changes.

Socioeconomic characteristics and mortality levels are also examined in relation to these natality trends. As predicted, it was found that natality declines in the Latin American region, especially since 1950, have been much faster than in northwestern or southern Europe. Furthermore, the Latin American countries that have experienced natality declines have tended to be those with relatively high levels of development and low levels of mortality, as posited by the theory. On the other hand, cross-country differences in rates of natality decline within Latin America are hard to explain in terms of rates of change in development or mortality. It is suggested that these problems result from the pronounced acceleration in all of these rates of change over time. Finally, the cultural factor is found to be closely associated with the timing and occurrence of natality decline. This effect seems to operate mainly through an intervening impact on the timing of development and mortality decline, but there also seems to be a direct effect of certain aspects of culture. This direct relationship is rather complex, however, and its influence seems to be attenuated as development is achieved.

Chapter 7 contains findings of the cross-sectional-longitudinal regression analysis. All hypotheses relevant to this section were supported. Socioeconomic development and mortality decline have their assumed (lagged) impact of reducing natality. Also as posited, greater land availability, economic expansion rate, and improvements in general mortality are associated with higher birth rates. The model as a whole, however, predicts that these effects should eventually be counteracted by socioeconomic development and long-term mortality trends. Chapter 7 also includes experimentation with cross-lag regression coefficients, autocorrelation problems, lag times, and forms of relationships. Although the full potential of these techniques is not realized, future promise for more sophisticated statistical methods is indicated.

Chapter 8 reviews the major findings and presents the most important conclusions of this research. There is considerable support for demographic transition theory in data pertaining to the Latin American region. Predictability is improved, however, if other variables known to affect natality are included in the model. Also, it is necessary to make some assumptions about lag times and forms of causal relationships. It is suggested that more sophisticated methodologies are appropriate for further research, provided that their use is guided by theory and the findings are carefully interpreted. The favorable results obtained in this study argue for the wider application of such methodologies in macroscopic sociodemographic research.

1 The Theory of the Demographic Transition: Background and Logical Status

Introduction

The historical background of the theory of the demographic transition is examined in this chapter, with the purpose of putting problems currently faced by the theory in perspective. The theory originated as a means of explaining European demographic trends that did not accord with accepted Malthusian ideas, and this in itself accounts for some of its present difficulties.

The second aim of this chapter is the development of a more systematic statement of transition theory. For the moment there is no attempt to modify the theory, but only to summarize those basic arguments which can be considered a macroscopic sociodemographic theory.

The Malthusian Model

The work of Thomas Robert Malthus has continued to stimulate demographic theorizing and research for over 150 years. In a sense his contribution was a negative one, since other writers, from Marx to contemporary demographers, have mainly been interested in refuting his theory, at least in its more simplistic versions.

Malthus asserted that the size of a human population is ultimately limited by "positive" or "preventive" checks. The former include "war, disease, hunger, and whatever . . . contributes to shorten the natural duration of human life" (Malthus, 1803:14). The "preventive" check is abstinence from sexual relations, accomplished either by delay of marriage or continence within marriage. Malthus then made the crucial assumption that the preventive check could not operate effectively without the threat of misery. Thus Malthus concluded that good living conditions for the majority of mankind implied unchecked population growth.

Malthus estimated that a population could double every twenty-five years. Although the exact figure is not crucial, his calculation was reasonably accurate. By contrast, Malthus asserted that food supplies in the long run could increase only in an arithmetic progression. This leads directly to the "Malthusian dilemma": with good living conditions, populations grow rapidly, but eventually the food supply is overtaxed until either the threat of misery forces use of the preventive check or else the positive checks intervene by increasing the death

1

rate. The eventual result is always population equilibrium and human deprivation.

There are two distinct propositions upon which Malthus constructed his argument: an assumption about the determinants of natality, and an assumption about the rate at which food supplies can increase. The theory of the demographic transition deals only with the former, by suggesting a new set of conditions under which natality can be checked. Only this aspect of the Malthusian model is discussed below.

Anomalous Empirical Trends

Class and Natality

Malthus himself came to recognize the growing evidence that the birth rate could be limited by voluntary means in the absence of severe deprivation (Malthus, 1836:436 ff.). This discovery seems to have stemmed from the observation that the upper socioeconomic classes had lower natality than others. By itself this fact probably did not suggest much reason for hope, since the upper classes were a distinct minority; however, Malthus contended that it might be possible to diffuse such admirable behavior patterns to the poor, and recommended universal education to accomplish this end (Malthus, 1836:437, 477). In recognizing the importance of class and education, Malthus was coming to appreciate the social determinants of natality. This is in contrast to his earlier formulation, which stressed biological processes and simple economic ideas. Although based on empirical observations, the inverse class-natality relationship detectable in his time was rather flimsy evidence to have so softened the gloomy pronouncements of Malthus's early writings. Malthus's thinking seems to have been affected as much by criticism he received, especially from Godwin (Petersen, 1971), as by his own research findings. However, as time passed, what must have appeared to him as a very minor trend grew to become a striking empirical reality.

European Natality Trends

It is ironic that Malthus presented the first edition of his *Essay on Population* (Malthus, 1798) at the very time when its assumptions were ceasing to hold in Europe. It is doubly ironic that the theory of the demographic transition, which arose to explain the divergence from Malthusian behavior, was not really formulated until those anomalous demographic trends were virtually complete in northwestern Europe. Theory has thus followed in the wake of empirical observations of European nations. This leads us to consider the demographic trends that came to be known as the demographic transition.

By 1800 mortality had fallen substantially in the more developed areas of Europe, generally in the northwest. This was contributing to a slow (by present standards) but persistent population growth, which presumably aggravated the concerns felt by Malthus and others. Gradually, however, scattered natality reductions became evident and by 1875 the trend was established throughout northwestern Europe. By 1900 birth rates all over Europe, with the exception of Russia and some of the eastern and southern extremities of the continent, were dropping. By the time of the Great Depression natality in western, central, and northern Europe was low enough to be at the point of long-term equilibrium with mortality, which itself was leveling off at a life expectation (at birth) of about seventy years. Although there were subsequent fluctuations, birth rates remained low in these areas. In eastern and southern Europe, including Russia, both mortality and natality decline lagged behind, so that the decline of the birth rate was not completed until fairly recent times. In a few isolated areas, particularly Albania, natality was still high, but falling, in the 1960s. Reductions in death and birth rates are among the most persistent and readily observable aspects of social change in nineteenth- and twentieth-century Europe. (See Kuczynski, 1928, 1931, and 1936 and United Nations *Demographic Yearbooks*, 1949-70.)

In its most elementary form, the theory of the demographic transition does not try to explain these trends, but simply summarizes them and labels the resulting empirical generalization the "demographic transition." Even at this stage the ideas have some empirical import. They assert that a substantial mortality decline invariably precedes and is inevitably followed by a major natality decline. This might be characterized as a phase theory, because it outlines three sequential stages of demographic development: initially, high and fluctuating mortality balances high natality; next, declining mortality coupled with high natality produces rapid growth; and finally, natality drops to roughly balance mortality and continues to fluctuate while mortality is relatively stable (Thompson, 1929; Coale and Hoover, 1958:12-13). However, demographers have not been content with mere description and, while theory construction has not been systematic, a theory has arisen nonetheless.

From this point one could either move directly to theory-building or else develop more detailed empirical generalizations. Demographers have done both, and while this discussion stresses the former, a few of the main empirical regularities are noted below in conjunction with theoretical development.

Common demographic patterns suggest that the values and norms governing natality are difficult to change. The tendency of mortality decline to precede natality decline is widely, but not universally, accepted (Stolnitz, 1964). Stolnitz (1964) has also indicated that future departures from high natality in non-European countries are likely to be slow in coming, and to lag well behind mortality reductions.

It has also been suggested that natality decline comes first to those parts of society most exposed to new values. This may account for early natality declines among upper classes (Cowgill, 1963). By the same token, it has been suggested that urbanites should have reduced natality sooner than rural persons, and in fact have done so. Although often considered a proven fact of the European experience, this latter assertion has recently been disputed (Carlsson, 1966).

Finally, the irreversibility of natality decline is another very important empirical finding based on the experience of European peoples (Stolnitz, 1964). There may be subsequent fluctuations of natality and at times these may be rather great in magnitude, such as the postwar natality recovery in Western nations. In the longer term, however, natality remains low, and in no case has it ever returned to pretransition levels. The arguments used to explain the demographic transition attempt to explain this and other empirical regularities referred to above.

The Theory of the Demographic Transition

Social Structure and Demographic Behavior

It was always obvious that the demographic transition was associated with the process that is variously called "modernization," development," "socioeconomic development," "bureaucratization," "industrialization," "urbanization," "progress," etc. Although early references to this association tended to be quite casual, a theoretical explanation was beginning to take shape and to become more detailed. The first statement of these ideas is usually attributed to Thompson (1929—see also Carr-Saunders, 1936).

The term "socioeconomic development" is often used quite carelessly, and left undefined. This book uses a standard, although rather broad, definition of "development" (which will also be referred to as "socioeconomic development" or "modernization"). It is assumed that the transition from a traditional agrarian to a modern urban society has several identifiable aspects upon which most social scientists would agree. Thus urbanization, rising levels of production and consumption, emergence of the money economy, advances in education, growing importance of social relationships and institutions not based on kinship, increasing secularization of life, and the shift from normative to functional integration are all aspects of development. Although each of these, and others that might be included, is a phenomenon in itself, they are interrelated (Ness, 1970), and there appears to be a common core, or a "common factor," which makes the term "development" meaningful. One or more dimensions of this process can arise independently, but ultimately all must occur if a society is to change, and this transformation is facilitated if all aspects are moving more or less together. These assumptions, if allowed, make it possible to speak of socioeconomic development in the broad sense. Note that, for reasons soon to become apparent, falling mortality levels have not been treated as part of the process. For the purposes of this study it is advantageous to consider mortality as a separate phenomenon, associated with development but not a part of it. However, there is no theoretical reason to consider it any more independent of development than some of the other types of social change outlined above.

Explaining Mortality Decline

The present study is concerned with natality, but a few comments about the transition-theory explanation of mortality decline are in order. The factors accounting for the decrease in the death rate are often considered nonproblematic. Furthermore, there is no real contradiction here between transition theory and the Malthusian model. It is usually assumed that individuals and cultures value life under most circumstances, and will seek to prolong it. They are therefore not hesitant to apply the technology of death control as it improves during development. Similarly, they are not reluctant to avail themselves of the increasing food supplies that are generated by the modernization of the agricultural sector. This improves nutrition and health and thus reduces mortality. There has been considerable debate among demographers over which factors (e.g., personal and environmental hygiene, public health measures, vaccination, food supply) were most important in lowering mortality at various periods (Helleiner, 1965). Some writers have even suggested that mortality could not have declined as early as was previously believed, and thus could not have accounted for the increased rate of European population growth observed in the early nineteenth century (Habakkuk, 1958; Petersen, 1960). In what follows, these problems will only be considered to the extent that they impinge directly on natality trends.

Explaining Natality Decline

Natality and Social Change. This book is concerned with natality, and in particular with those factors that are associated with natality decline during socioeconomic development. It is in this area that transition theory has made its greatest and most original contribution while stimulating research and theoretical discussion.

Malthusian thinking inextricably linked "good times" with high birth rates. On the other hand, the experience of the demographic transition in Europe suggested the opposite—in terms of wealth, education, social reform, health, and in almost every conceivable way life was generally becoming more pleasant and comfortable all the while the birth rate was falling to levels never before recorded except in periods of dire distress. It has been noted that Malthus became aware of the possibility of such behavior after observing class differentials. As early as 1864, Mill (1864:205-12) recognized that whole societies were beginning to control natality consciously, apparently to protect their rising standard of living—at least this was his interpretation. Mill not only magnified the cautious optimism of the later Malthus, but went on to anticipate the relationship between socioeconomic development and natality control, while suggesting an explanation for it. Later, when the European natality decline was largely past history, many other explanations were proposed, and despite their variety and lack of coherence, all of them are generally considered to be part of the theory of the demographic transition.

The Role of Contraceptive Technology. Although it is widely agreed that socioeconomic development is somehow responsible for natality decline, there has been some disagreement as to how and why this comes about (Robinson, 1964). Early explanations tended to stress the increasing availability of modern contraceptive devices that accompanies development (Carr-Saunders, 1936:105 ff.; Fairchild, 1939:127-51; Bogue, 1967). Critics of this approach pointed out that traditional means of birth limitation, such as coitus interruptus, are often available long before socioeconomic development, and that these methods, while unreliable at the individual level, can reduce the aggregate birth rate considerably. They also noted that the major portion of the European natality decline antedated the widespread use of modern contraceptives (Notestein and Stix, 1940:148 ff.). Thus, one would be hard put to explain why the French birth rate dropped almost continuously from the Napoleonic period onwards to the 1930s on the basis of contraceptive technology. Most demographers have taken the more tenable view that contraceptive technology is a facilitator rather than the basic cause of the natality decline associated with development (Robinson, 1964:385).

The Role of Values, Norms, and Mortality. Other explanations proposed that the cause of the modern decline of natality was to be found in "new patterns of living and new values" (Notestein and Stix, 1940:149-50). Changing values, occupational and residential composition, and increasing education were specifically mentioned by these authors. Under the heading of "values" Notestein and Stix pointed out that development tends to weaken the traditional fatalist orientation, and thus leads people to feel that many aspects of their lives, including natality, can be regulated. They suggested, as Malthus had, that education helps to spread the new attitude throughout society. They also regarded urbanization as a multifaceted cause of reduced birth rates; urbanism tends to foster a more highly skilled and better educated work force, which tends to make the laboring class more similar to the upper classes. It was also suggested that urban women are less restricted by traditional sex roles and are more often employed outside the home (Notestein and Stix, 1940:148 ff.). Stolnitz (1964:33-34) pointed out that the employment of women means that their lost wages and/or the price of child care must be added to the economic cost of children. What is outlined above, then, is a sociodemographic theory of sorts. Changes in values and social structure are linked, more or less clearly, to falling natality. This orientation takes the early class differentials in natality very seriously, and tends to assume that the motivation and ability to control births diffuses to the lower classes as they acquire some of the benefits, social attributes, and values once confined to the upper classes.

One of the persistent problems of transition theory is that various authors make essentially similar arguments but stress different points or use different terminology. For instance, economic terms can often be substituted for sociological concepts or used in conjunction with them. Thus development may cause natality decline partly by raising the cost and lowering the economic value of children (Coale, 1969). A sociologist could also point out, however, that the adoption of prohibitions against child labor, a normative change, is a part of this process, or it could be suggested that it is a decline in the *status* value of large families that is crucial (Davis, 1963). Similarly, one could argue that rising status of women results in a greater opportunity to choose some role other than wife-mother for a greater portion of the life cycle. When value changes are involved, the confusion extends even further. Various authors have stated that natality falls partly because of the emergence of "nonfatalist" attitudes (Cowgill, 1963), "nontraditional" values (Stolnitz, 1964), "secular-rational" attitudes (Coale, 1969), "work orientation," and "individualism" (Clifford, 1971). Although the many shades of meaning and terminologies can confuse presentations of transition theory, the fact that so many different approaches lead to similar formulations is encouraging. An interrelated nexus of social, economic, and psychological changes that accompany socioeconomic development makes large families far less desirable for parents.

The declining importance of kinship structures that accompanies development has often been accorded a special theoretical position in the explanation of natality decline. In traditional societies, extended kinship systems help to place a high social and economic premium on the bearing and raising of large families (Lorimer, 1954:58-90, 151-203). As development occurs, the importance of extended kinship systems is reduced by the growth of other institutions, and the nuclear family becomes the basic family unit. Freedman (1963) has developed this general argument further by noting that the process involves participation in larger, more specialized institutions; in fact he defines "development" as "the shift from major dependence on relatively self-contained local institutions, to dependence upon larger social, economic, and political units." Freedman (1963) suggested that this places the social and economic costs of children more directly on the parents, and at the same time makes more than a small number of children irrelevant to the "goals men seek in the more developed society."

Some, but not all, authors have postulated that mortality decline itself causes natality reduction (Freedman, 1963; Coale, 1969). This mechanism has usually been viewed as somewhat distinct from the impact of socioeconomic development, although mortality is associated with development. It is usually argued that with lower infant and child mortality, fewer births are necessary to assure a given ultimate family size. Thus, with high mortality many births might be required to guarantee with reasonable probability that one son will survive to support his parents in their old age. Unfortunately, this idea, which is sometimes called the concept of "insurance births," makes an implicit assumption about rationality. It seems to imply that persons, even in traditional societies, have some fairly specific ideas about the ideal or desirable ultimate family size, and that they take mortality into account when deciding how many children to have.

There is another way of explaining the causal link between mortality and natality, however, which does not put so much of a burden on the individual. The lowering of infant and child mortality without offsetting birth control can greatly increase household size, and play havoc with social structures designed to accommodate lower survivorship (Freedman, 1963:226-27). One example is inheritance systems—arrangements that may have been serviceable in the past may become hopelessly overloaded when too many children survive to adulthood. This can be especially crucial when it is land that is involved. Thus, if individuals control their natality in response to lower mortality, it may be the result not of an understanding of demographic trends and their implications, but of a simple defensive reaction to the burdens of families larger than existing social and economic structures can readily handle.

Organizing the Theory as It Pertains
to Natality

The above factors can be grouped on the basis of causal priority and the type of motivation through which they are assumed to operate. First it is generally agreed that socioeconomic development is the basic cause of natality decline. This covers at least four interrelated phenomena: urbanization, education, nonkinship institutions, and consumption levels (standard of living). These are said to facilitate intervening modifications of individual behavior via social, economic, and/or psychological mechanisms. The social cluster includes the relaxation of sex-role restrictions on women, the decreased predominance of extended kinship systems, and the reduced status value of children, especially male heirs. The central factor certainly seems to be kinship—as development proceeds, formal organizations based on secondary association take over many of the economic, educational, and political functions previously served by kin groups. Economic variables of importance include the reduced labor value of children, the increased cost of raising children, the emergence of competing consumer goods, and the money value of the wife's labor outside the home. Psychological factors are more difficult to enumerate, since attitudinal changes can be expressed in many ways, but the following orientations seem to facilitate natality decline—nonfatalism, materialism, rationality, and secularism.

Usually these variables are thought to mediate between socioeconomic development and "desired or ideal family size." The latter are hypothetical constructs which appear, though often implicitly, in most explanations. This is not a necessary assumption; even in developed societies family size is not always the result of planned, conscious decision. Of course this problem can be avoided by making "desired or ideal family size" a norm, and thus avoiding the assumption of individual decision.

Mortality is also assumed to affect natality, but without any apparent impact on the *ultimate* family size desired or thought to be ideal. Rather mortality, especially that of infants and children, is thought to mediate between ideal-desired family size and the practice of birth control. (This assumption will be modified in a subsequent chapter.)

Finally, natality decline is caused by the implementation of some type of birth control. This in turn is affected by desired-ideal family size and mortality levels, although, following arguments made above, it is typically assumed that birth-control technology has an independent, but not overriding effect. Delay of marriage or abstinence from sex might also be viewed as means of birth limitation.

Trying to illustrate such a system with even a primitive causal diagram is very difficult, since almost every set of variables might potentially affect every other. Nevertheless a crude attempt is made below (Figure 1-1). This model does not pretend to be complete, but only a summary of some of the major relationships suggested by transition theory.

Transition theorists generally portray causation as moving from the upper left to the lower right. We cannot, however, rule out feedback. Some of these possible "reverse" relationships are indicated by the double-headed arrows, but even these do not exhaust the conceivable complications. For instance, it is very probable that natality itself affects the development variables, that desired size affects birth-control technology, etc. These relationships are excluded from the diagram for the sake of legibility.

In general, the theory of the demographic transition is not well explicated, but is weighted down with numerous supplementary arguments drawn from different disciplines. The only clear implication of the theory is the prediction that socioeconomic development will lead to natality decline, and that this will tend to occur sometime after a major decline in mortality.

The Demographic Transition as a
Sociodemographic Theory

The theory of demographic transition is not a set of logically interrelated propositions from which testable empirical statements can be formally derived. Nevertheless, it does make empirical assertions and propose causal arguments.

10

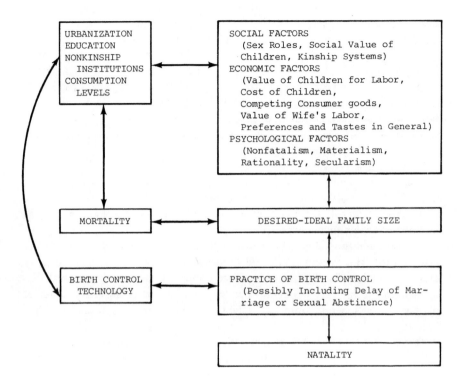

Figure 1-1. Causal Model of Demograhic Transition Theory

Some versions of the "theory" are in fact empirical generalizations. However, if one thinks of these generalizations as predictions of what "should" happen in societies that have not yet experienced the demographic transition, then one begins to have a theory of phases of demographic movements. The present transition theory also consists of explanations of the above empirical regularities. At the first level this simply involves the notion that socioeconomic development reduces the birth rate, but more detailed arguments are incorporated to explicate the relationship between socioeconomic structure and natality. Unfortunately these additional arguments are not always complementary or cumulative. Rather, each more or less independently attempts to make the development-natality-decline association plausible. Since the theory arose specifically to explain the previously anomalous natality declines, this tendency is understandable, but little seems to have been added to precision or the predictive capacity in the process.

The Theory of the Demographic
Transition as a Paradigm

Disappointment with the theory should not obscure its great contribution. Sometime between the first and most simplistic version of Malthus and the statement of the theory of the demographic transition, a great discovery was made: Natality is a function of economic, social, psychological, and cultural factors. Despite its shortcomings, the theory has provided a framework for the scientific study of human natality, and we might consider whether the "theory" is in fact a paradigm.

Thomas Kuhn (1962) has discussed the nature and import of scientific paradigms at some length. He states that a paradigm is attained after some striking breakthrough that is sufficiently unprecedented to attract an enduring group of adherents, solve some major problems, and yet be "sufficiently open-ended to leave all sorts of problems for the . . . practitioner to resolve" (Kuhn, 1962:10). Often such a paradigm arises in reaction to a set of data, anomalous relative to previously existing theory.

The theory of the demographic transition fits Kuhn's criteria fairly well. The theory did arise after an anomalous series of events—the European natality decline. The Malthusian model could not explain what was happening, so the way was cleared for new ideas. The real "breakthrough" consisted of linking social change with demographic change and proposing new sociological, cultural, psychological, and refined economic arguments to further explain the connection. Previously these factors were not clearly recognized as causes of natality. The theory of the demographic transition not only suggested that they were, but also indicated how and in what directions they ought to operate. It can be argued, of course, that the so-called "explanations" were not logically tight, and certainly that the theory was and is not as determinate as theories typically found in the natural sciences. Kuhn (1962:27-34) points out, however, that even Newton's classic theoretical work *Principia*, and many other efforts of similar stature, were rough and cumbersome in their initial statement. It required a great deal of reformulation and revision to bring these theories to the elegant and articulate level at which we now encounter them. If the explanations of the various statements of the theory of the demographic transition are not rigorous, they are at least plausible in the light of modern social science. In any case, the most important function of the theory has been making further demographic research possible by telling investigators what variables to consider and what relationships are reasonable. According to Kuhn, this is the primary function of a paradigm, for it makes what he calls "normal science" a viable enterprise (Kuhn, 1962:35-42).

The theory's weakness, both as a theory and as a paradigm, is that it leaves too much unstated and too many ideas unintegrated. It still requires a great deal of refinement. Unfortunately, demographers have often been more interested in finding an exception to some of the empirical generalizations more or less implied by transition theory than in improving the logical structure. For this reason and others, the paradigm suggested by transition theory has remained rather crude.

Specific Problems Currently Faced by the Theory

Recently there has been a resurgence of interest in transition theory, for at least three reasons. First, there has been an unprecedented increase in world population, due largely to declining mortality in the developing areas. Second, conditions in these nations now seem to resemble in certain respects those which preceded the massive natality decline in Europe. Third, quantitative data are increasingly available to measure not only demographic variables but also many aspects of socioeconomic structure. Circumstances thus seem ripe for a refinement and extension of the theory, once we have summarized its current problems.

Most difficulties arise from the disagreement among investigators as to the content of the theory. This is understandable, since the theory has certain aspects of an empirical generalization, a true sociodemographic theory, and a paradigm. A given datum may support, or be irrelevant to or inconsistent with the theory, depending upon how it is interpreted. For the present we will use the model presented in Figure 1-1 and the ideas underlying it as a guide in determining the predictive capacity of transition theory. (This model still needs to be made more explicit and testable; this is done in a subsequent chapter, after analyzing the empirical results of other investigators.)

Sometimes the theory is faulted incorrectly because it is interpreted as the most simplistic empirical generalization. The mere fact that the particular demographic trends previously observed in Europe are not found elsewhere does not disprove the theory, but this is often taken to be so. The theory itself should not, as a theory, predict that the same trends of the dependent variables will occur everywhere, but only that the predicted *relationships* with the independent variables will hold true.

On the other hand, the fact that the theory has certain characteristics of a paradigm sometimes leads researchers to expect too much of it. No social theory will explain all salient features of a dependent variable. The theory of the demographic transition does not claim to exhaust all the possible determinants of natality, but only to isolate some strong relationships that were responsible for major trends in the past. Since the theory was formulated with the object of explaining the demographic trends in nineteenth- and early twentieth-century Europe, probable determinants of natality that did not help explain these particular trends did not receive much attention. This does not imply that other causal factors are negligible or that transition theory is wrong in leaving them out. It does warn the researcher that the independent variables embedded in transition theory may not completely determine natality.

The increasing popularity of statistical analyses has also resulted in some difficulties for transition theory. A regression or any other mathematical model represents some kind of hypothesized system. Given that many researchers do not know what the theory of the demographic transition states, they run a serious risk in using a mathematical model to test it. Standard mathematical procedures will give sensible answers only to questions that are appropriately posed. Unfortunately, some investigators have forsaken theory completely in favor of a blind regression of natality on a variety of measures, some socioeconomic and some demographic, without any consideration of the assumed causal system.

It is hoped that in what follows, some of these problems can be alleviated or avoided while the theory is revised and refined. This new model will then be tested with data from the Latin American region. However, for the moment the theory will be left as it stands, a partially explicated theory linking socio-economic structure, mortality, and natality. In the next two chapters empirical experiences of both Europe and the more recently developing areas will be examined. It is to be hoped that this will help to indicate the ways in which the theory must be altered.

2 The Demographic Transition in Europe

Introduction

More demographic research has focused on Europe than on any other area. This chapter does not attempt a comprehensive review of the literature that deals with European social and demographic transition. For detailed historical accounts, the reader is referred to the articles cited throughout the chapter, especially to works by Coale (1969), Demeny (1968), Flieger (1967), Habakkuk (1958), Kirk (1946), Livi Bacci (1968a, 1971), Petersen (1960), Slicher van Bath (1968), Spengler (1938, 1968), and Van de Walle (1968).

Since the theory of the demographic transition was formulated with the European experience in mind, one would expect the theory to explain that behavior rather well. As indicated below, this is only partly true. One reason for difficulty is the great attention that has been paid to northwestern Europe, to the exclusion of other parts of the continent. Furthermore, research is continually uncovering new facts not previously known. Thus, transition theory encounters anomalies even in explaining the demographic trends in Europe.

In this chapter, considerable attention is directed toward findings that seem to challenge transition theory. The analysis is selective, in that the topics chosen are of general theoretical interest and applicable to later chapters in some way. The fact that the European experience *in general* supports transition theory is assumed, and only a short section is devoted to documenting this argument.

Empirical Problems for the Theory

Controlled Natality in the Pretransition Period

One of the more common and well-documented findings in European historical demography is that of rather low natality in the pretransition period. Before socioeconomic development really began,[a] natality was being limited by forces other than biological capacity. This holds for most of Europe, with the possible exception of the eastern regions (including Russia). Several writers discuss this point, and conclude that natality was limited by relatively late marriage and

---

[a]Obviously certain aspects of development had been under way in Europe very early. However, general socioeconomic development (including such processes as industrialization) did not really gain momentum until the late eighteenth century or even later in most areas.

probably deliberate birth control as well (Freedman, 1963; Hajnal, 1965; Leasure, 1963; Livi Bacci, 1966, 1968a, 1968b, 1971:48-79; Petersen, 1969:383-84; Spengler, 1938).

It is not entirely clear that the existence of relatively low (less than maximum) natality or even the widespread use of birth control preceding socioeconomic development is a refutation of transition theory. Early versions of the theory did tend to assume or implicitly suggest that deliberate birth limitation is unique to modernized society (Thompson, 1929; Fairchild, 1939:105ff.); however, this was never a crucial idea. In explaining why natality falls as development proceeds, the theory does not need to assume that traditional societies seek maximum natality. The general observation that the birth rate was only moderately high in pretransition Europe (except the eastern part) is not a serious problem so long as natality dropped considerably further after development began. This is one case in which an apparent contradiction is not really a serious threat to the theory. Transition theorists have tended to concentrate on the trends they felt were problematic—the declines in the vital rates, especially natality. In the process, some of them may have made unwarranted assumptions about other phenomena. The misunderstandings that have then arisen illustrate the fact that the theory of the demographic transition has often been confused with a global theory of human natality.

The theory attempts to isolate independent variables that explain the major natality declines of the demographic transition. During other periods, natality trends may be dominated by other determinants of natality. This is not damaging so long as the variables in the theory *do* determine the major trends in natality during the main phase of socioeconomic development, and natality is relatively high before the transition but low afterwards.

The real significance of controlled natality in pretransition Europe is the implication that there are rather *powerful* determinants of natality in addition to those discussed by transition theory. There have been many suggestions as to which factors account for these relatively low birth rates. Certainly late marriage limited natality, but one must then consider the reasons for late marriage.

Shortage of usable land is often advanced as an explanation of late marriage and/or low birth rates during the agrarian period in Europe (Demeny, 1968; Livi Bacci 1968a, 1968b, 1971:48-79). Certainly the only part of Europe to experience really high birth rates in the immediate pretransition period was the east, which was not fully settled (Coale, 1969). The inability to find farms capable of supporting a family is bound to discourage early marriage. In some cases the social structure may reinforce this tendency by requiring dowries or bride prices that insure that a newly married couple will have access to means of support, and in an agrarian society support comes from the land. If land is scarce, it may be necessary to wait until an inheritance can be claimed or until enough wealth is acquired to purchase a farm, and the result is delayed marriage. In some cases, postponement of marriage may even reach its extreme form of celibacy. Persons unable to obtain land may choose to enter some alternative occupation, such as the priesthood or the military (Livi Bacci, 1968b, 1971:52, 131), which is not as compatible with family life as farming. While land does seem to be an obvious explanation for depressed natality in agrarian societies, the complexity of the relationship should be stressed—one must consider not only the supply of land but the effective availability of usable land to the ordinary person. The distribution of land is a very important consideration, since much land is often held by a few powerful persons and may be unavailable to the great majority. On the other hand, an improvement in agricultural tech- nology acts like an increase in the supply of land, by reducing the acreage needed to grow a given amount of food. For example, Hofstee (1954) points out that population growth in The Netherlands was associated with both improve- ments in fertilizers and seeds and actual increases in arable land achieved by diking and filling. It is also necessary to consider the role of social structure in mediating the effects of land supply (Lorimer, 1954:151-203). Inheritance practices, e.g., primogeniture versus more equal division of land, and the norms governing bride prices and dowries are clearly important. Finally, one must examine the existing alternatives to farming. In truly agrarian societies there are probably few other opportunities, but as urbanization begins the situation can change rapidly, and the probable impact of land supply on natality could diminish.

There are other potential explanations of the limitations on natality during the pretransition era in most of Europe, but these tend to be made specifically for a given area and are difficult to generalize. Among the more widely applicable factors cited are religion and health. Livi Bacci (1968b) and Goubert (1968) have suggested that a strong Catholic Church in the Iberian countries and Brittany, respectively, actually depressed natality by encouraging an unusual prevalence of celibacy. As noted above, however, it is possible that this is partly a secondary effect of land scarcity. Goubert (1968) also points out that poor health can impair fecundity, and attempts some demonstration that this had a significant impact in Brittany, resulting in natality lower than in parts of France that had better nutrition and environmental hygiene.

As already noted, the existence of determinants of natality not discussed by transition theory does not refute the theory. In fact, realism demands that there be other important variables. One must know something about these other factors, especially the more powerful ones, in order to make predictions about natality. Since predictions are needed to test theories, a fair test of transition theory ultimately requires some control for the effects of independent variables that play no central role in the theory itself.

The Timing of Natality Decline

Irregularities Within Specific Nations

There are several cases in which natality decline is said to have begun first in areas of a country that were not the most developed. Each country of Europe could be examined, of course, and no doubt irregularities could be found in any of them. Rather than attempt such an extensive analysis, this discussion focuses on the general problem and draws examples from countries in which the theory seems to encounter the most difficulty.

Probably the best-documented instances of early natality declines in relatively rural and underdeveloped subnational areas are in Portugal (Livi Bacci, 1971), Spain (Leasure, 1963; Livi Bacci, 1968a, 1968b), Hungary (Demeny, 1968), and France (Goubert, 1968). These examples fall into two types: those in which the author supplies an explanation outside the scope of transition theory, and those in which the theory seems to have been misinterpreted.

Demeny (1968) and Goubert (1968) give explanations for early natality declines in less developed areas of Hungary and France respectively. The main arguments, as stated above, involve growing pressure on the effective supply of land and, for France, poorer health in rural areas. Again these factors do not represent a direct contradiction of transition theory; they are simply other variables that affect natality.

Livi Bacci (1968a, 1968b, 1968c, 1971:55-79, 101-24) has attacked transition theory more directly on the basis of his study of the Iberian peninsula. He states that both southern Spain and southern Portugal combined early natality decline with levels of development that were low or moderate even by their own national standards (see also Leasure, 1963). He makes this case much more clearly for Portugal, for which he presents historical series of development, mortality, and natality data.

Livi Bacci's argument depends on the assumption that northern Portugal was at least as developed as the south, and that this should imply that natality decline should begin in the north before or at about the same time as the south. While northern Portugal was as developed as southern Portugal on the basis of most indicators, mortality was consistently higher in the north. Since mortality is accorded a special place in transition theory, it should be treated as a more powerful determinant of natality than any single development indicator. Thus, the higher mortality of the north would lead to the prediction of higher natality. The fact that natality did fall first in the south is then quite understandable in terms of the theory. It should be noted, however, that Livi Bacci (1971:127) emphasizes the more secular attitude of the south, and suggests that this encouraged early natality decline while the more religious north retained high natality. This is a possible alternative interpretation of the data, but ideas such as "secular attitude" have been considered part of transition theory in the past and cannot constitute a rival theory.

Livi Bacci's work brings out one very important point: The various aspects of development and mortality decline do not change in lockstep fashion. It is possible for some of these to change faster than others in various areas. Since transition theory is not particularly explicit about handling the several independent variables, the theory will not always be able to make clear predictions;

this is a real theoretical difficulty, but not an empirical refutation. On the other hand, the theory does accord mortality a special position, and this should be taken into account.

Irregularities in Cross-national
Comparisons

Again there will be no extensive analysis of the relationship of timing of natality decline and development-mortality levels in every European country. Rather, this section deals with a few countries in northwestern Europe, where the national comparisons seem most inimical to the theory. Specifically, two nations that did not seem particularly developed by about 1875—France and Ireland—began natality decline very early, while two of the most industrial—England and Wales and The Netherlands—maintained high natality relatively late. (Germany was in many ways similar to England and Wales in having rapid industrialization and relatively late natality decline. Germany is not discussed in this section mainly because its modernization began later, and the shift in time periods would considerably complicate the argument to be made. Most of the observations made here concerning England and Wales would apply fairly well to Germany if the time dimension were taken into account. The German case would suggest the same theoretical and methodological points as the English experience.)

By the middle of the nineteenth century, England and Wales had emerged as the most industrial and urban nation, and The Netherlands, while less urban, was an important commercial center and had a gross national product not far behind that of England-Wales (Clark, 1957; Spengler, 1968). Estimated 1870 national product per capita in 1963 U.S. dollars was $463 for The Netherlands and $626 for England-Wales (International Bank, 1970). By contrast, France was still largely rural and had a lower gross national product of $351 per capita in 1870 (Sundbarg, 1908; International Bank, 1970). Ireland was much worse off, being an economically and socially underdeveloped society in most respects (Sundbarg, 1908).

France's birth rate began to drop in the Napoleonic period, and continued to decline consistently until the 1930s. In Ireland a natality decline began about 1850. At first this trend was associated with the potato famine and heavy emigration, but since it was sustained it must be regarded as the major natality decline of the demographic transition. By contrast, the birth rates in both England-Wales and The Netherlands peaked about 1870, and did not begin to fall convincingly until around 1875. Thus, the expected associations between development indicators and natality trends do not seem to materialize. The question is whether this is a real problem for transition theory. There are two major issues to be considered.

First, urbanization, national product, and commerce are not the only aspects of development, and the theory stresses the importance of mortality indicators. These other independent variables help to explain the case of France and, to a lesser extent, Ireland. In terms of education and literacy, France was either close to or ahead of England and Wales and The Netherlands *circa* 1900. The illiteracy of military conscripts in all these countries was under 5 percent, but in school enrollment France was ahead (Sundbarg, 1908)—the percentage of the population between the ages of five and fifteen in school was estimated at 90 percent in France, versus 82 percent in England and Wales and 70 percent in The Netherlands about 1900. Even lowly Ireland, far behind in most other respects, had 80 percent of the population in this age bracket in school in 1906. Mortality levels, to the extent they can be measured, seem to have been about equal in all four of these countries in the late nineteenth century, with the number of annual deaths per 1000 persons being 23.6 in France, 22.5 in England-Wales, and 25.4 in The Netherlands during the 1860s (Sundbarg, 1908). The apparent death rate in Ireland for this time was 20.5, but this is said to have been about 10 percent too low, due to incomplete death registration (Sundbarg, 1908:112); this correction would put the rate almost equal to that of England and Wales. These other variables do not explain the natality trends observed, but they do make the pattern of natality decline less anomalous in terms of the theory. Unfortunately, earlier comparative data are not available.

A second major consideration, and one not always taken into account, is the lag time assumed by the theory. If natality trends are caused by socioeconomic and mortality changes sometime in the past, then it is not proper to examine contemporaneous values of these dependent and independent variables. If natality trends in the late nineteenth century are at issue, socioeconomic and mortality data at some earlier period should be examined. Unfortunately, as one goes further back in history, the availability and quality of socioeconomic and mortality data decrease, and it is not the purpose of our investigation to make an intensive study of the scattered data that can be obtained for the early nineteenth century. However, France was probably the leading country in Europe about 1800. Furthermore, the spurts of economic growth that boosted England and Wales and The Netherlands ahead of other countries seem to have occurred in the middle and latter portions of the 1800s (Sundbarg, 1908; International Bank, 1970).

The above argument suggests two main points. First, development does have various aspects, and if the theory is to be applied, some effort must be made to measure these. The several facets of development are not perfectly correlated in every country at every time. Second, an accurate test of the theory also requires some kind of lag time between socioeconomic change and natality decline. Results that otherwise appear to contradict the theory can sometimes be made compatible with it, depending on how development is measured and what (if any) lag times are allowed.

Natality Increases During
Socioeconomic Development

In some countries there seems to have been an increase in natality even though development was clearly under way. The best-documented case is probably England and Wales (Habakkuk, 1958; Krause, 1957; Wrigley, 1968), but similar findings are reported for The Netherlands (Hofstee, 1954; Van de Walle, 1968). Furthermore, Friedlander (1969) points out that there was a secondary peak in the crude birth rate in Sweden occurring after natality decline was apparently well under way; this is especially interesting, because Sweden is often thought to typify the demographic transition in Europe.

The strictest interpretation of transition theory could dismiss the above problems by assuming that the theory is not concerned with minor reversals of trend. However, the present interpretation of transition theory does assume a monotonic inverse relationship between socioeconomic development and natality. If natality does sometimes rise during development, other explanations (outside transition theory) must be found, or else the fundamental ideas of the theory must be questioned.

It is particularly disturbing that the countries with the clearest indication of natality rise, England and Wales and The Netherlands, were among the most rapidly developing nations of Europe during the nineteenth and early twentieth centuries. It is conceivable that the rapid growth of industry and accompanying urbanization actually removed prior restraints on natality. Such restraints could have been motivated by the limited supply of agricultural land and translated into behavior by means of the social structure of the traditional agrarian society. The growth of industrial cities could have eliminated the restraining effect of land, and simultaneously disrupted the social structure that had previously acted to limit births. There are several findings that suggest that expansion of industry per se may raise birth rates. Even the industrial (northern) parts of France had higher birth rates than other sections of the country (Goubert, 1968). Furthermore, improvements in the standard of living might have continued to encourage rather high natality. At some point the theory must address such apparent contradictions.

Empirical Support for the Theory

While this chapter stresses problematic findings, some attention should be given to the considerable evidence that supports the theory. Three points are dealt with here. First, there is no country that represents a clear refutation of the theory. Second, there was a close association between natality and development-mortality, both longitudinally and cross-sectionally. Third, rates of development and mortality decline correspond in a general way with rates of natality decline.

In every instance in which a European country modernized and reduced mortality, a natality decline followed. In all of Europe only Albania now has high natality; there development and mortality decline were also late in coming, and the birth rate is currently falling rapidly. There are very few, if any, social theories that have no major exceptions. The most general prediction of transition theory, however, is never violated within Europe.

The pattern of natality decline suggests a diffusion process (Carlsson, 1966; Coale, 1969), but actually follows the trends of development and mortality decline. Each of these changes came first to northwestern Europe and then moved to the south and east (Kirk, 1946:36-72). Thus, at any particular time between about 1875 and 1930 there is a strong cross-sectional association between development-mortality levels and natality. While there are always a few areas that upset the trend, in general the relationship is quite close.

Finally, rates of natality decline are associated with rates of development and mortality decline, at least among the major subregions of Europe. Generally speaking, all of these trends moved at a moderate pace in northwestern Europe. The two countries with slow natality decline, France and Ireland, also underwent rather slow development. Italy's experience was similar to northwestern Europe, although social and demographic change came slightly later. The Iberian nations, however, encountered slow progress in development, mortality reduction, and natality decline. Finally, as social and demographic change proceeded across Europe, rates of change accelerated. Thus in central Europe the processes moved faster than in the northwest, and in Russia and eastern Europe the acceleration was even more pronounced. In each case, the associations among rates of development, mortality decline, and natality decline are generally in line with transition theory. Data on socioeconomic development and mortality decline may be found in Kuznets (1964), Kuczynski (1928, 1931, 1936), International Bank (1970), Sundbarg (1908), and United Nations *Demographic Yearbooks* and *Statistical Yearbooks*. Table 2-1 shows rates of decline in crude birth rates in various areas of interest.

Summary

A close examination of the European experience reveals certain problems for transition theory, while confirming its most general predictions. The difficulties that arise include theoretical, methodological, and empirical issues.

The theory of the demographic transition fails to specify certain assumptions that must be made if meaningful research is to be carried out. Thus, it does not clearly state what aspects of development should be measured or how long lag times should be. Although the theory does treat mortality in a special way, it is clear that most theoreticians assumed that mortality decline was closely linked to development, and hence it was not necessary to consider what might happen if they moved more independently. Furthermore, the theory does not overtly

Table 2-1
Average Annual Declines in Crude Birth Rate in European Countries

Area of Country	Period	Rate of Decline
Northwestern Europe, mean	As listed below	.26
Northwestern Europe, mean (excluding France and Ireland)	As listed below	.30
Belgium	1875-1935	.28
Denmark	1885-1934	.31
England and Wales	1876-1934	.37
Finland	1876-1934	.32
France	1876-1938	.15
Ireland	1875-1939	.09
The Netherlands	1876-1936	.26
Norway	1878-1935	.29
Scotland	1875-1939	.29
Sweden	1876-1934	.28
Switzerland	1876-1938	.27
Southern Europe, mean	As listed below	.25
Italy	1884-1953	.29
Portugal	1923-1970	.23
Spain	1885-1954	.24
Central Europe, mean	As listed below	.39
Austria	1875-1936	.35
Czechoslovakia	1875-1937	.41
Germany	1875-1932	.42
Hungary	1883-1963	.39
Eastern Europe, mean	As listed below	.44
Bulgaria	1906-1966	.49
Poland	1898-1967	.35
U.S.S.R.	1897-1967	.47

Note: The national rates of natality decline are from Kirk and Beaver (1971). The methods by which the calculations were made are the same as those described in Chapter 6, section on hypotheses. National territories are of date except as listed: Austria and Hungary are present territory; Czechoslovakia is western Czechoslovakia; Poland is the "Central Provinces" as defined by the interwar government; U.S.S.R. before World War I is the fifty provinces of European Russia.

state its units of analysis. In this vacuum, individual researchers have had to make their own assumptions, and transition theory can often be made to appear either confirmed or refuted depending upon exactly how it is operationalized.

The theoretical shortcomings also contribute to existing methodological problems. It is difficult to obtain data on certain aspects of development. As a result, measures of national product per capita are sometimes equated with development. Measurement is much easier if it is assumed that all aspects of development and mortality decline are perfectly correlated, but this is not the case. It is also hard to obtain data from earlier periods, and this hinders consideration of the lag times required by the theory—hence the tendency of investigators to forget the lags entirely.

Nevertheless, there are some real empirical problems. Clearly there are variables not discussed in the theory that affect natality. This point must be conceded, and the most important of the other factors should be taken into account in making predictions. In addition, certain aspects of the development process seem to create a tendency for natality to rise temporarily especially if natality was relatively low in the pretransition period. In view of the data and the plausible rationale for this effect, it should be considered explicitly, since it calls into question a fundamental assumption of the theory.

3

The Demographic
Transition in Non-European
Societies

Introduction

Demographers have been understandably dubious about making predictions for non-European societies on the basis of the theory of the demographic transition, which was formulated with the European experience in mind (see, for example, Arriaga, 1970b and Weller and Sly, 1969). In this chapter research on non-European populations is utilized to evaluate transition theory predictions. Excluded from this analysis will be the overseas extensions of Europe, such as the United States and Canada.

We begin with the unique case of Japan, the first non-European society to become developed and the first to experience the demographic transition. The rest of the Third World is then considered. Finally, special attention is given to studies of the Latin American region and to the relevance of that area's somewhat unusual demographic history for transition theory.

Japan

Natality and Development Trends

Records of vital events in Japan were notably incomplete until the twentieth century. By 1920, when dependable official statistics became available, the birth rate had evidently dropped considerably (Tsubouchi, 1970). Hanley's analysis (1968) does suggest, however, that population control was practiced very early, especially by means of infanticide (usually of females) and abortion. In the Bizen Province, on which Hanley concentrates, there were apparently successive periods of population increase and decrease from 1679 to 1738, although it is not clear to what extent these were caused by variation in the birth rather than the death rate. Hanley (1968) links the period of population growth with expansion of arable land through reclamation, irrigation, and drainage, and with advances in fishing, trade, and small-scale manufacturing. These suggest an easing of pressure on the land and a favorable economic climate. Although the information on early Japanese demographic history is woefully incomplete, it does seem that, as in most of Europe, natality in the pretransition period was well below "uncontrolled" levels. Furthermore, in both instances it seems as though favorable conditions are associated with population expansion—a finding more in keeping with the Malthusian model than transition theory.

The major natality decline in Japan seems to have begun in the late nineteenth century. It is estimated that *circa* 1875 the gross reproduction rate was about 3.0 (Taeuber, 1960), higher than most western, northern, central, and southern European societies at the beginnings of their respective natality declines but lower than rates estimated for Bulgaria and Russia around 1900 (Kuczynski, 1936), and certainly lower than "uncontrolled" levels. From this time on Japan made great socioeconomic progress, and reduced both mortality and natality. Although we cannot be certain of the details, it does seem as though socioeconomic development and major reductions in the birth rate were closely associated in Japan. The fact that this occurred "naturally" in Japan— i.e., this was before the days of effective family-planning programs—suggests that transition theory is not inherently limited to European culture, and must therefore be considered a major victory for the theory.

Regional Variation

At least two investigators have found that regional variation in Japanese natality also favors transition theory. Taeuber (1960) used the proportion of the population in industry or agriculture as an indication of development. Cohort analysis gives retrospective information about past differentials. This method revealed a strong contemporaneous association between high levels of development and relatively low birth rates, which had apparently been present at least as far back as 1920.

Tsubouchi (1970), using historical records, reached similar conclusions. Correlations in the expected direction are found between the proportion of the population in agriculture and natality, and this also holds for changes in these variables. Tsubouchi (1970) also found that infant mortality was positively correlated with natality, although not very closely—he attributes the low value of the correlation coefficient to the rather low observed variance in regional infant mortality, a valid methodological point. On the other hand, Carlsson (1966) cites Japan as one instance in which the regional variation that is taken to confirm transition theory was actually present before socioeconomic development was under way. This casts some doubt on the above findings, but, even if true, would not be a definitive refutation of transition theory. It is possible that the differentials in the pretransition period, as in Europe, were caused by a different set of factors, later replaced by the relationships predicted by the theory.

Rates of Natality Decline
and Development

The rapid rates of development in Japan are almost legendary. This trend has been most pronounced since World War II, but was present even before then.

Muramatsu (1967:12) estimates that between 1920 and 1940 real per capita gross national product increased at an annual rate of 3.4 percent. This compares quite well with the impressive 3.7 percent figure observed for the Soviet Union—a nation which also began development from low levels around the turn of the century. Nor is this progress confined to economic variables. In many respects Japan was one of the most developed nations by 1960. Furthermore, mortality decline was quite rapid, taking place in about forty years. In the thirty years between 1930-34 and 1960-64 alone, the female expectation of life at birth rose 23.3 years, from 48.2 to 71.5 (United Nations, *Demographic Yearbooks*).

This fast change in the independent variables of transition theory is matched by a very precipitous natality reduction. From 1920 to 1960 the crude birth rate declined .44 point per year on the average. Again this is close to the observed rate for the Soviet Union, .46 point per year (see Table 2-1).

The experience of Japan supports transition theory. As in Europe, factors not considered in the theory seem to affect natality in the predevelopment and early development periods. But in the long run the theory does well. Development and morality decline lead to natality decline, and rates of change in the former anticipate those of the latter.

The Developing World as a Whole

Findings According to Successive Partitions of the Sample

Dependence of conclusions on the nature of the sample. The major empirical problem to be resolved is whether the posited development-natality relationships can be found more generally in the developing regions. The studies reviewed below are cross-sectional regression analyses that employ many development indicators as independent variables and some natality measure as the dependent variable. Nations are typically the units of analysis, but various researchers have used different samples, and findings seem to be a function of this choice.

It is quite easy to obtain high correlations between development measures and birth rates if one includes all the nations of the world with appropriate data in the sample (United Nations, 1963). Such findings really demonstrate that European societies, including overseas areas of European settlement, and Japan have lower birth rates and higher socioeconomic development than less-developed nations. In one striking demonstration (United Nations, 1963) it was found that the association between development and natality virtually disappeared when the sample was partitioned into more- and less-developed societies—within these groups correlations were close to zero. This could be taken as a setback for transition theory; however, very little theoretical analysis of the result was made at the time.

Other studies that also partition the world into less- and more-developed subsamples do find relationships between development and natality (Adelman, 1963; Friedlander and Silver, 1970). Since each investigator uses different methods and measures, such contradictory findings are common. Nevertheless it is clear that relationships observed in a world sample do change when only less-developed countries are examined. The problem is to assess the theoretical import of this phenomenon.

Theoretical ambiguity of developed nations. Transition theory makes no unequivocal predictions about differentials within the more developed group. It surely asserts that these nations should have low birth rates, as they do. It does not seem realistic to say that the theory predicts that the inverse development-natality relationships will go on indefinitely. There is clearly a "floor" effect on natality. For this reason alone, the natality-lowering impact of development must eventually end, or at least approach zero. In fact, since World War II some of the world's most urban and wealthy societies have had relatively high birth rates (e.g., the overseas extensions of Europe in the United States, Canada, Australia), although still much lower than those of underdeveloped societies. On the other hand, the lowest natality in the world can often be found among nations that are the least developed of the more developed group—e.g., Bulgaria, Hungary, Rumania. There is a temptation to explain these observations in terms of such factors as political ideologies, accessibility of abortion, availability of housing, or immediate economic well-being. This suggests that in the posttransition era, as in pretransition times, factors other than level of socioeconomic development again become the dominant determinants of natality. In other words, we are reminded that transition theory seems to be limited to one phase, albeit an important one, of development, and that it is not a complete theory of natality behavior.

Enigmas in less-developed nations. Within the less developed group, failures to consistently obtain the inverse development-natality relationships are more damaging to the theory. *If* these areas are in the range of development theoretically associated with secular natality decline, transition theory should predict the inverse relationships. A disturbing characteristic of the theory is that it avoids specifying such particulars as what this range should be.

Empirically, even a superficial review of the principal developing regions suggests why difficulties occur. For a developing region, mainland Latin America generally enjoys high literacy and per capita product, and is rapidly urbanizing; mortality fell rapidly and has been relatively low for years. Despite all this, Latin America, except for its temperate regions, has had very high birth rates. By contrast, east and south Asia (except Japan) have generally had more modest levels of development, although mortality is now near that of Latin America. Nevertheless, birth rates in southeast Asia (notably India and China) have been relatively low for a developing area. Other major regions are not quite so enigmatic. The Islamic world combines low development with high birth rates; the West Indies region has moderate development and moderate natality levels. Finally, sub-Sahara Africa seldom figures in empirical work, because of poor data. The picture is mixed but we can see why results can be perplexing.

The notion of cultural regions. Another research strategy (Kirk and Srikantan, 1969; Kirk, 1970) has gone further, and partitioned the developing world into Latin America, Islam, southeast Asia, and India. (The other logical regions, sub-Sahara Africa and China, lack usable data.) Examining these groups of nations separately has the effect of dramatically reviving strong development-natality relationships in the expected directions. The researchers' explanation for this and justification for their methodology is the need to seek more culturally homogeneous samples than the "developing world." They have suggested that socioeconomic development might not affect natality in quite the same way in all societies, and that different aspects of development might be more important to lowering the birth rate. They feel that by controlling for gross cultural differences much of this nonuniformity is eliminated.

In terms of the sizes and signs of the cross-sectional correlations within regions, this idea has certainly been vindicated. More interestingly, the particular variables most closely linked to natality differ by region and the pattern has been suggestive. In Asia, historically an impoverished and crowded area, measures of per capita product have been more effective in predicting natality decline than elsewhere (Kirk, 1970). In the Islamic nations, education has seemed to be more crucial—understandable in view of the traditional Moslem views regarding Western-style secular education, especially for women. In Latin America, social communication or societal "infrastructure" variables (e.g., telephones per 1000 population) were found to be most closely related to the birth rate. Although the interpretation is a bit less clear in this case, it appears that the extent to which Latin American societies have modern institutions linked in some way into a national system is the crucial characteristic. Other empirical support for this regional approach is provided by Janowitz (1971), who found that dummy variables for regions entered into a cross-sectional regression had important effects on natality, even with transition variables controlled.

Although the above approach has been quite successful, some difficulties remain. If the ideas of these authors were accepted *and* incorporated into transition theory, that body of thought would become more complex and inelegant. We would have to build in the ill-defined concept of "culture" in order to derive a prediction about development and natality.

Defenders of transition theory might wish to integrate culture into the theory as a measurement problem. In other words, a given indicator such as education of women, urbanization, or national product might not *mean* the same thing in different cultural regions. Departure from the traditional socioeconomic structure is theoretically important in every region, but the most sensitive measure of this change could be different across cultural regions. This is an interpretation of the Kirk-Srikantan (1969) and Kirk (1971) findings that accepts their validity but would not consider them theoretical complications, but rather improvements of measurement. It would preserve the simplicity or the original transition theory, while leaving it up to investigators to determine what best measures "departure from traditional socioeconomic structure" in a given culture.

Conclusion: The effect of variously partitioned samples. The conflicting findings produced by examining different samples of countries reflect the fact that researchers either are not consciously testing transition theory or do not know how to operationalize it accurately. The observation that some impressive relationships have been found with certain subsamples does lend credence to the basic ideas of transition theory. It is particularly noteworthy that the development-natality association, which is problematic within the sample of all under-developed societies, reappears with more strength than ever when these societies are again divided into broadly homogeneous cultural regions. Unfortunately, the notion of cultural region has an uncertain and presently inelegant theoretical meaning. Continued theoretical development could alleviate this problem (see Kirk, 1966, 1971).

Findings for Specific Independent Variables

It is also instructive to examine the many cross-national studies that regress natality on development measures without regard to the particular samples used. One must remember, however, not only that different samples are employed, but also that independent variables, assumed forms of relationships, measures, and strategies for dealing with measurement error and multicollinearity, among other things, differ greatly among these studies. In view of these circumstances and the relative lack of guiding theory, it is a wonder that any uniformity among the findings survives. In fact, there are often conflicting results, but the research suggests a definite pattern that has important theoretical implications.

Certain transition theory variables do tend to yield consistently confirmatory results. Infant or child mortality is usually found to be positively related to natality despite great differences in sample and methodology (Friedlander and Silver, 1970; Heer, 1966; Weintraub, 1962), and often to be a relatively powerful determinant. Similarly urbanization—or its complementary concept, proportion of the population engaged in agriculture—and education, indexed by school enrollment or literacy, generally demonstrate the predicted relationships with natality, and occasionally one or the other emerges as notably powerful

(Adelman, 1963; Adelman and Morris, 1966; Friedlander and Silver, 1970; Janowitz, 1971). Mass communication measures such as newspaper circulation or radios per 1000 population are less routinely included, but have been found to be negatively related to birth rates as one would anticipate of any development indicator (Adelman and Morris, 1966; Friedlander and Silver, 1970; Heer, 1966).

Per capita income or product is by far the most enigmatic transition theory variable. It occasionally displays a positive association with natality (Adelman, 1963; Heer, 1966; Weintraub, 1962), the reverse of other development indicators. Of course this represents the effect that remains after other independent variables, including development measures, are partialed out, but it is still an interpretive problem.

This "income-reversal" effect does not seem to survive if the sample is limited to developing nations and the observed relationship with natality becomes either negative or insignificantly small (Adelman and Morris, 1966; Friedlander and Silver, 1970; Kirk and Srikantan, 1969; United Nations, 1963). It is only among the most developed nations, which are presumably beyond the demographic transition, that a strong positive income-natality relationship emerges (see also pp. 27-29).

In dealing with the interpretation of the income findings, Heer (1966) makes a distinction between the impact of short- and long-term changes. It is well established that the former generate a positive natality-income association—this has been referred to as a "business-cycles" effect, and reflects the tendency for birth rates to fall during depressions and recessions and to rise during times of expansion (Basavarajappa, 1971; Galbraith and Thomas, 1941; Hexter, 1925; Hyrenius, 1946; Kirk, 1960; Silver, 1965). The long-term income effects are opposite in sign and can be equated with the transition theory prediction. Clearly it is now possible to assume that the short-term process is dominating posttransition areas while in the developing world both may be present, although the long-term effect seems to be more prominent, as we would expect in view of the hypothetical potency of the massive socioeconomic change indicated. Heer (1966) demonstrates empirical support for his position by showing that, even among developing nations, changes in per capita product (or energy production) are positively related to natality.

Heer's analysis (1966) also leads him to a fundamental methodological critique of most cross-national studies. He notes that if a high birth rate at time 1 has a deleterious impact on development at time 2, as is often assumed (e.g. Ohlin, 1967), and the birth rates at times 1 and 2 are closely related, then observation at time 2 alone will tend to build in a spurious negative relationship between development and natality (see Figure 3-1). Since the same argument can be made for changes in any development measure, such as per capita product, Heer concludes that the positive associations he obtains for increases in per capita product and energy production are actually mitigated by the lagged

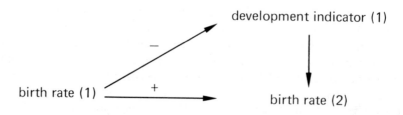

Figure 3-1. Model of Income-Natality Relationship

natality effect, and hence underestimate reality. More important, Heer's criticism affects all of the cross-sectional research supporting transition theory, since any negative relationship between natality and a development measure (or a positive relationship for a mortality measure) could be the spurious result of effects of lagged natality. This is a potential threat we deal with in Chapter 7.

Another criticism that can be directed at most of the cross-sectional results supporting transition theory involves an examination of the unstandardized regression coefficients obtained. Janowitz (1971) found that her coefficients gave highly unrealistic natality predictions, if one assumes changes in independent variables similar to those of transition-era Europe, or indeed almost any plausible pattern. This poses an additional quandary, since much, if not all, of the cross-sectional research that tends to confirm transition theory might tend to refute it if projected along a likely longitudinal trajectory of socioeconomic development.

Finally, some investigators have included independent variables beyond those suggested by transition theory. In general these efforts have failed to produce results that are both substantively and statistically significant, but these unfavorable findings can prove instructive. Perhaps the most intuitively interesting variable is population density, which might be interpreted as an operationalization of land scarcity, at least in predominantly agrarian societies. The less-rigorous European research previously reviewed (Chapter 2) hinted at a major rule for this variable. Unfortunately multiple regression analyses suggest that population density has a very minor impact on natality (Friedlander and Silver, 1970; United Nations, 1963). These problems might, however, be due to contradictions of measurement: population density might also be correlated with urbanization, especially in smaller countries, and this may obscure its operation as an index of land scarcity. Other variables that have been included in multivariate analyses and found to have negligible influence on natality include linguistic homogeneity (Friedlander and Silver, 1970), and the existence of political parties, dominance of the military, and nationalism (Adelman and Morris, 1966), among others.

Despite all the difficulties and the occasional failure to obtain favorable results, the research tends to confirm the negative relationship between development and natality among countries of the developing world. It also suggests that the relationship may at times be exaggerated or obscured by other factors that affect natality but are not controlled. At this point, procedures have been too crude to determine how precise and dependable the causal link between natality and development is. However, the fact that exact answers have not been found with some of the more obvious tools of methodology does not mean that those answers do not exist.

Latin America

Overview

The empirical section of this volume will apply a respecified version of transition theory of Latin America. Therefore, special attention is paid to previous work focused on that region. In many respects Latin America seems to be an enigma for demographic theory, and the positions taken by various investigators differ considerably.

The Cultural Regions Approach

This approach (Kirk and Srikantan, 1969; Kirk, 1971) undoubtedly ranks as one of the most optimistic views of the applicability of transition theory to Latin America. As already noted, Kirk and Srikantan (1969) find high correlations in the expected directions between various indicators of development and natality within the Latin American region. Countries were the units of analysis and crude birth rates the measure of natality. Despite the success of this study (see Table 3-1) these results are somewhat suspect, because the development indicators were selected from a larger group for predictive purposes. Nevertheless, almost anyone would have to admit that the observed correlations are impressive.

In an effort to supplement the Kirk-Srikantan (1969) findings and to ascertain the relationship between general development and natality in Latin America, I sought a broadly based development measure that had been devised without any immediate concern with demographic issues. McGranahan's Development Index (McGranahan, 1971) fits the criteria and was available for sixteen Latin American countries *circa* 1960. The correlation between this index and gross reproduction rates *circa* 1963 was found to be $-.680$, certainly in the desired direction and reasonably high, although lower than all but one of the correlations obtained by Kirk-Srikantan (1969). Despite this mildly encouraging result, a plot of the observations (Figure 3-2) displayed relatively little relationship between development and natality in the lower three-fourths of the development distribution. This seems to reinforce the earlier conclusion that it is

Table 3-1

Zero-Order Correlations Between Crude Birth Rate and Eight Development Indicators in Latin America

Crude Birth Rate Correlated with:	r
% of population in places 20,000+	−.752
% of economically active males in agriculture	−.852
% literate males ages 15+	−.676
% literate females ages 15+	−.722
telephones per 1000 population	−.937
daily newspapers per 1000 population	−.797
hospital beds per 1000 population	−.831
females' life expectation at birth	−.756

Note: Countries used were Argentina, Barbados, Chile, Colombia, Costa Rica, Cuba, Dominican Republic, Ecuador, El Salvador, Guatemala, Guyana, Haiti, Honduras, Jamaica, Mexico, Nicaragua, Panama, Paraguay, Peru, Puerto Rico, Trinidad and Tobago, Uruguay, and Venezuela. Data are *circa* 1962. If the necessary assumptions for the usual test of statistical significance are made, all of the above correlations are significant beyond the 1% level.

Source: Kirk and Srikantan (1969).

difficult to predict natality in the early stages of development, but that in the long run natality decline dependably follows development. These findings do not necessarily mean that the Kirk-Srikantan (1969) results are merely produced by selectivity of development indicators—the indicators they put forth may be genuinely more sensitive or associated with critical aspects of development. Nevertheless, qualification is required before asserting that there is *in general* a strong relationship between development and natality in Latin America.

Other Regional Studies

Heer and Turner (1965) performed a cross-sectional analysis of smaller, subnational units in Latin America and report much different, more complex results than those reported by Kirk-Srikantan (1969). Possibly this could be due to the units of analysis or to the peculiarities of the variables utilized. The only natality measure available for the many subregions of Latin American nations was the child-woman ratio, an index that builds in child mortality, and is hence questionable, due to the fact that child mortality is itself related to development. The independent variables include the usual variety of development indicators, but these are split into those describing the immediate local characteristics of the particular area (local) and those referring to the whole society (national).

35

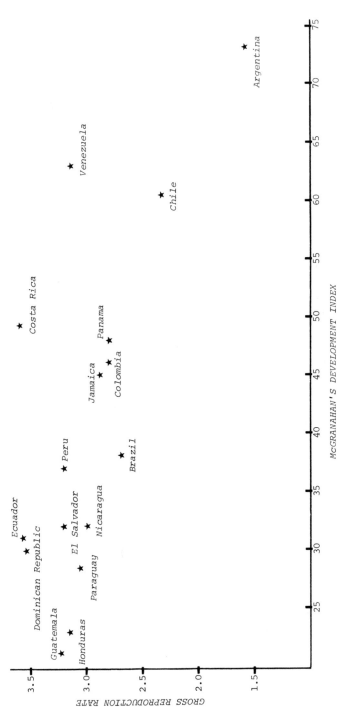

Figure 3-2. The Relationship between Overall Development and Natality in Latin America about 1960. Notes: Development data are *circa* 1960 while natality data are from *circa* 1963. The observed correlation between the two variables graphed is −.680; although we do not defend the application of significance tests in cases such as this, the correlation would be significant at the 1% level if the necessary assumptions were made. Sources: McGranahan (1971); United Nations (1963); and United Nations *Demographic Yearbooks*.

The best predictor variables are local female labor force participation, local urbanization, and national literacy—all are quite reasonable measures of development, and all are related in the expected direction to the child-woman ratio. However, in a few nations local relationships are consistently the reverse of that expected. Furthermore, some variables, notably the national percentage of economically active males in agriculture and local literacy, are associated with natality in the "wrong" directions, even in the whole sample.

In attempting to explain these inconsistencies, Heer and Turner (1965) cite the experience of Spain as characterized by Leasure (1963), who asserts that weak or reverse natality-development relationships were not uncommon there. This is in keeping with the anomalies noted in both Iberian nations by Livi Bacci (1968a, 1968b, 1968c, 1971). These authors suggest that agricultural people often have both the motivation and the ability to limit births—perhaps even more than urban people at some stages of development. Furthermore, the improving economic conditions associated with development may tend to encourage higher natality in all sectors of society—this is quite similar to the argument later repeated by Heer (1966) and discussed above. To test the latter idea, Heer and Turner (1965) construct a measure of the rate of recent economic expansion and find that its correlation with natality across all subregions is +.51. Although strong and in the expected direction, this relationship is notably absent in several nations where other factors seemed to have been more crucial in determining natality. In general, this study finds some support for transition theory and proposes that, where exceptions are found, they may not be dissimilar to what occurred in southern Europe, a culturally related area.

Stycos (1968) has made an extensive analysis of Latin America natality at the national, regional, and individual levels of analysis. He, too, finds that at the national level development-natality relationships are generally as predicted by transition theory. Using urbanization, female employment, and family status (including the existence of common law or "consensual" unions), Stycos (1968) finds that urbanization is the most important factor in natality decline, embodying as it does many of the aspects of development and yet persistently adding a unique component of explained variance despite the application of controls (Stycos, 1968:236-88). For other independent variables, however, the application of controls sometimes reverses within-country regional correlations (Stycos, 1968:278).

A more original but less quantified portion of Stycos's work (1968: 215-35) deals with the transition from Indian to Spanish mestizo culture. He feels that this trend may initially raise birth rates, by encouraging more stable sanctioned sexual unions. This argument is reminiscent of Goode's suggestion (1961) that in Latin America the change from traditional to modern society includes a period of relative disorganization during which kinship controls of sexual relations and presumably procreation are likely to be lessened. Heer (1964) confirms this hypothesis in finding that Indian-speaking (traditional) areas of the Andes usually have lower natality than nearby Spanish-speaking areas.

Stinner (1969) also analyzes Latin American natality at the regional level. Stinner's independent variables include not only development indicators, such as female literacy and urbanization, but also "intermediate" variables, such as the prevalence of consensual unions and delay of marriage, which should relate to the culture-kinship argument made by Goode (1961), Heer (1964), and Stycos (1968). The independent variables are assumed to affect natality according to four different causal structures with which the author experiments. The dependent variable in this study is child-woman ratio corrected by infant morality—a potentially good measure if the "corrections" are reasonably accurate.

Stinner (1969) reports that choice among the causal models makes little difference to the findings. As with Stycos (1968), urbanization is found to be an important factor in reducing natality, operating not only directly but also through literacy and by encouraging female labor force participation. Findings for other variables support transition theory except that, as in the Heer and Turner (1965) study, literacy, here female literacy, sometimes has a positive association with natality when other variables are controlled. Stinner tries to account for the reversal by suggesting that at low levels of development small degrees of progress can raise natality via such demographic mechanisms as higher fecundity, lower fetal mortality, and greater survivorship of fertile couples as reproducing units, as well as other mechanisms such as perception of expanded opportunities for one's offspring and one's own enhanced ability to care for them.

Another part of the Stinner (1969) research deals with the intermediate mechanisms of postponed marriage and consensual unions, and points out a divergence between Stycos (1968), and Heer (1964) and Goode (1961). Although all three of these authors assert that one can anticipate a temporary rise in natality in Latin American societies, they disagree as to timing. Stycos (1968:215-35) believes that natality will rise as the norms and values of European culture cut down the number of consensual unions and create more stable unions. The other two authors suggest that the maximum natality should be intermediate between the traditional native culture and the acceptance of the European (Iberian) values in the reintegrated mestizo culture—in other words, the period of maximum birth rates coincides with the time during which consensual unions would be expected to be common, the period of disorganization between the destruction of one culture and the institution of a new one. Stinner (1969) supports the latter view by reporting that the effect of many consensual unions is to raise the birth rate (controlling for direct effects of development).

Marital postponement is also more prevalent in the least- *and* the most-developed countries of Latin America (Stinner, 1969). This finding again indicates that the highest natality would be expected to occur during the period of maximum disorganization. Following Heer (1964) and Goode (1961), it appears that the traditional societies maintain controls over sexual behavior and marriage, probably through the kinship structure, but that these controls break down with the disruptive impact of social change. Finally, as development moves further, a new normative structure emerges that encourages delay of marriage (or at least childbearing), but now with the help of widespread birth control.

The "Non-European" Critique

Finally, there is another line of thinking about Latin America that more actively challenges transition theory, stressing the region's deviance from the so-called "European" model. Authors who adopt this attitude perceive the Latin American experience as a disconfirmation of transition theory and an indication that the theory is culturebound (Arriaga, 1970b; Forni, 1970). Basically, this argument asserts that except for the more European nations of the region (Argentina, Chile, Uruguay, and possibly Cuba) Latin America has persisted in high natality despite the fact that mortality is now quite low and has been falling since at least 1930.

Arriaga (1970a, 1970b) has demonstrated rather convincingly that mortality has dropped much faster in Latin America than in Europe—although his exact figures are in question, the magnitude of the differences he discovered is too great to ignore. He argues that mortality decline in Latin America has been effected by what anthropologists would probably call diffusion—in this case the self-conscious implementation by government agencies of death control technology "borrowed" from other cultures. Arriaga feels that socioeconomic change has not been needed to drastically lower mortality, and that the fundamental cause of the European natality decline is therefore absent. He infers that a fall in the birth rates of most Latin American societies is likely to be much delayed at best.

Although Arriaga makes his position quite clear, its theoretical import is not apparent. The fact of an unusually rapid or premature mortality decline in Latin America does not necessarily refute the basic ideas of transition theory. Under such circumstances, transition theory should predict exactly what Arriaga himself anticipates: delayed natality decline. As noted previously, it would be naive to expect the actual trends of birth and death rates to be similar in all developing societies. Arriaga's idea of the "European experience" seems to be a straw man version of transition theory. He never actually denies that socioeconomic development lowers natality, but instead states that mortality decline has been relatively independent of social change in Latin America. Transition theory was not really intended to handle such an eventuality, since mortality decline was closely connected to socioeconomic progress in Europe. However, it is clear that most theorists believe that it is basic social change and not mortality decline alone that lowers birth rates.

A more persistent difficulty for the theory originates from the fact that socioeconomic development *has* been proceeding at a rapid rate in Latin America, and has already attained relatively high levels (UNESCO, *Statistical Yearbooks*; United Nations, *Statistical Yearbooks* and *Demographic Yearbooks*; Vries and Echavarria, 1963). Comparable data on per capita national product for both postwar Latin America and pre-World-War-I northwestern Europe are displayed in Table 3-2.

It can be seen that the rate of expansion of the Latin American economies, even in per capita terms, has been comparable with that realized in the best long period of development in northwestern Europe, 1880-1913. The comparison of

Table 3-2
Annual Rates of Growth of Real Per Capita Product and Real Total Product in Percent

Area	Period	Total Product	Per Capita Product	Type of Estimate
Northwest Europe[a]	1880-1913	2.6	2.1	Mean of national rates
Northwest Europe[a]	1880-1913	2.6	1.8	Mean weighted by 1900 population
Italy	1890-1927	1.9	1.2	National rate
Italy	1927-1960	2.7	2.0	National rate
Latin America[b]	1950-1960	4.5	1.9	Mean of national rates
Latin America[b]	1950-1960	5.5	2.6	Mean weighted by 1955 population
Latin America[b]	1960-1968	4.9	2.0	Mean of national rates
Latin America[b]	1960-1968	4.8	1.8	Mean weighted by 1965 population

[a]Belgium, Denmark, France, Germany, Netherlands, Norway, Sweden, Switzerland, United Kingdom.

[b]Argentina, Bolivia, Brazil, Chile, Colombia, Dominican Republic, Ecuador, Guatemala, Honduras, Jamaica, Mexico, Nicaragua, Paraguay, Peru, Puerto Rico, Uruguay, Venezuela.

Notes: An effort has been made to display the best long-term period experienced by northwest Europe and Italy during development. The slowing of economic growth indicated by the Latin American weighted average from the 1950s to the 1960s is largely a result of the Brazilian economy—expansion was truly remarkable during the 1950s, but slackened slightly in the period 1960-68. For Jamaica, the 1950-60 period is really 1953-60; for Uruguay, it is 1955-60. For Bolivia, the 1960-68 period is actually 1960-69; for Brazil, Colombia, Mexico, and Paraguay, it is 1960-67; for Ecuador, it is 1960-64; for Jamaica it is 1960-66. These peculiarities were dictated strictly by the availability of data in the source listed.

Sources: For Europe, Kuznets (1964) provides the national rates. For Latin America, the same data are given in various issues of the United Nations *Statistical Yearbooks*. Population estimates used in calculating the weighted means are from various issues of the United Nations *Demographic Yearbooks*, except for some of the 1900 figures, which were only available in Kuczynski (1928). A few of the 1900 data are actually for a nearby year.

Latin America with Italy, the most developed society in the culturally related southern European region, is even more favorable. When one considers that Latin America has had to deal with a rate of population growth more than twice as rapid as that of either northwestern Europe or Italy, its achievement is impressive.

The theoretical problem is a direct result of this apparent progress, which can also be documented, although not always so strikingly, in terms of education, urbanization, or almost any other common development index. Since transition theory states that development and mortality decline bring about lower birth rates, the theory would predict that natality should certainly decline soon if it has not done so already. It is even more perplexing that the most common trend of birth rates in Latin America during 1930-60 seems to have been upward (Collver, 1965). This enigma is considered in the theoretical model to be developed and tested in the following chapters.

4 A Respecification of the Theory

Introduction

In this chapter we draw on the lessons of previous theory and research in an attempt to further specify the theory of the demographic transition, to refine it, and to explicitly take into account certain "control" variables that may have been responsible for apparent refutations of the theory.

Levels of Analysis

The theory of the demographic transition has been articulated at many levels of analysis: individual, group, institutional, and societal. We are here concerned with the societal level, and set forth a theory that relates the social structure and less fundamental characteristics of societies to natality levels. Ways in which social change might be translated into the behavior of families, couples, and individuals are considered, but there are no specific hypotheses about these processes. The reader is referred to "The Ecological Fallacy," Chapter 5, for an explication and defense of this strategy. While societies are the theoretical units of analysis, the hypotheses, presented in the latter part of this chapter, refer to countries that are assumed to approximate the idea of "societies."

The Fundamental Assumption

As interpreted here, the theory of the demographic transition is essentially an aspect or a special case of the sociological theory of social change. It is concerned with the relationship between social and demographic change. Furthermore, it relates to the particular social change from some type of traditional, nonindustrial, usually agrarian society to a modern bureaucratic-urban society. In focusing on this phase of change, the theory is in the tradition of Weber's Protestant ethic, Durkheim's theory of functional and normative integration, and Parsons's pattern variables. In other words, the theory concerns one of the mainstreams of sociological inquiry. As it stands, the fundamental assumption of the theory is that societies that have modernized will for various reasons, sketched out in Chapter 1, have much lower natality than traditional-agrarian societies. This theme is now elaborated.

41

Family size is seldom directly controlled by formal negative sanctions, but childbearing is regulated in all societies, though sometimes in a fairly loose way. There are rarely rules calling for persons to have a specific number of offspring—the most obvious exceptions being those for whom having any children is proscribed, such as members of celibate orders, the insane, etc. For the ordinary person, social influences on natality behavior are more subtle but nonetheless powerful. All societies place some value on parenthood and attempt to influence it. Birth is the main source of "recruits" for any large society. Furthermore, a society cannot depend merely on biological drives to supply its new members because it requires socialized recruits who have a position in some kinship or family structure. Every enduring society must therefore value "proper" parenthood for a large majority of its "normal" adult members.

Some authors have found it useful to speak of the value of *children* per se, and to distinguish between economic and social aspects of value. It seems more reasonable to assume that it is the *role of parent* that is valued. Furthermore, it does not seem helpful to try to separate social and economic aspects of value, since these seem to be closely related causally as well as highly correlated empirically. It is true, however, that it is sometimes easier to use established economic theories to show how social change reduces the economic value of children than to use sociological theories to demonstrate a corresponding diminution of the social value of children and parental roles; this is probably more a commentary on the states of these disciplines than on underlying causal structure.

The nexus of values relating to parenthood and childbearing is considered a unitary phenomenon, obviously an oversimplification, and is referred to as the "values governing the bearing and socialization of children" or simply "values." Clearly these values may not be perceived the same way by all classes or persons but it is assumed that a society does have a distinct set of values that affects most of its members. It is also apparent that childbearing-parenthood values are often specific for parity and sex. Thus it is almost always important for couples to raise one or two children, including at least one male. The real differences among societies come at higher parities and in the character of the sex preference, which generally varies from strongly male to mildly male, with a supplementary value placed on having at least one child of each sex (Blake, 1965). Nevertheless, the values of some societies encourage their members to have more children than others—this is the crucial simplifying assumption. Finally, it is assumed that values have some impact on natality behavior.

This concept of values is intended to replace the idea of "desired or ideal family size" (see Figure 1-1). Although the new concept is analogous to the earlier notion, it avoids the implications of individualistic rationality conjured up by "desired or ideal family size." It also avoids the implication that the expressed attitudes of individuals are the ultimate measure of this crucial link of the demographic transition. Individuals cannot always articulate the value structure which directs their behavior (see Ryder, 1969). The idea of "values" also diverges from desired or ideal family size, in that it is not restricted to ultimate family size. Societies may value having many children partly *because* they tend to die prematurely. Thus the present conception of "values" is not necessarily independent of childhood mortality, a strategy which seems dictated by reality.

The fundamental assumption of the theory of the demographic transition can then be rephrased to assert that childbearing-parenthood values encourage natality much less in modernized societies than in any traditional society, e.g., agrarian, horticultural, hunting and gathering, etc. If a society changes, values and behavior should change accordingly. The mechanisms by which this process is thought to work have already been explored by transition theorists (see Chapter 1). The reduction of the importance of extended kinship systems tends to lessen the status value placed on numerous progeny and simultaneously to concentrate the physical and emotional costs of child-raising much more on parents. With socioeconomic development, alternative sex roles for women become more available and attractive. In urban societies the labor of children becomes less useful and children become a drain on family resources. As consumption levels rise and materialism becomes more acceptable, children must compete for time and resources with other activities and goods that are increasingly important for the maintenance of status. Meanwhile the opening of the class structure allows greater social mobility and enhances the importance of income and consumption as indicators of social rank; this also contributes to the competition for family resources that discourages large numbers of children. The differentiation of social institutions (e.g., economic and political structures) from the kinship system implies that some important roles filled by individuals are nonfamilial, and that the functions fulfilled within the family are reduced. These are the major causal mechanisms. They can be phrased in different terms and there may be others, but these are the factors that seem most crucial from a sociological perspective.

The simple assertion that developed societies have lower natality than traditional societies is not a very strong prediction. Researchers have typically gone on to assume that there is a monotonic inverse relationship between the extent to which a society has attained socioeconomic development and its encouragement of parenthood. This transforms a weak theoretical typology of societies into a very strong assertion relating the *process* of social change to that of demographic change. To be realistic, one has to limit the posited relationship to a segment of social change—societies continue to change and to modernize long after natality decline ceases, and even the most developed society places some value on the raising of children.

One other modification is usually applied to the fundamental assumption of transition theory. There is an assumed time lag between the basic processes of social change (urbanization, advances in education, rising levels of living, etc.)

and changes in values and the resultant natality decline. Theoreticians often posit a tendency for basic values to persist far longer than other aspects of social structure and culture when change occurs. One could interpret this as a version of Ogburn's "cultural lag" hypothesis (1922, 1955), which asserts that technology changes more readily than either social structure or culture, and eventually brings about changes in the latter. While this argument may be oversimplified, basic values are one of the more permanent aspects of a society. This position is consonant with Parsons's (1966) view of the stability of the "pattern maintenance" system.

At this point some consideration should be given to the so-called "intermediate variables" (Davis and Blake, 1956).[a] Values, in order to affect natality, must be translated into control over a biological process. Davis and Blake (1956) have constructed a well-known typology of ways of affecting the birth rate, both through self-conscious and involuntary processes. However, it does not seem useful in the present context to illustrate the ways in which values work through various intermediate variables. It is clear that modern societies tend to use contraception (listed under "exposure to conception" in the Davis-Blake system) as well as abortion (under the heading "gestation") in purposive attempts to control natality. It is also probable that some societies make significant use of voluntary abstinence ("exposure to intercourse within unions"). Furthermore, it is apparent that in some European societies (see Chapter 2) rising age at marriage ("age at entry into unions") was an important factor in reducing natality initially. Thus it appears that values can be implemented in a variety of ways, and it is unlikely that one could trace out a universally applicable pattern of causation in any coherent, useful manner.

Finally, there is a certain awkwardness in considering socioeconomic development a unitary phenomenon. Obviously it is many things. Nevertheless its identifiable aspects quite obviously depend on each other causally, and in any case they are highly intercorrelated (Ness, 1970). This is what gives the idea of development some coherence. Therefore, development is considered a single phenomenon but it is measured by three traditionally distinct aspects: urbanization, education-literacy, and levels of living. The final form of the fundamental assumption is then:

Assumption 1: Socioeconomic development of a society causes lagged changes in its value system which encourage progressively lower natality over some large range of development.

---

[a]There are eleven intermediate variables separated into four groups. "Formation and dissolution of unions" includes "age of entry into sexual unions," "permanent celibacy," and reproductive time after or between unions. "Exposure to intercourse within unions" includes "voluntary abstinence," "involuntary abstinence," and "coital frequency." "Conception" variables include fecundity as affected by voluntary and involuntary causes and contraception. "Gestation" variables include foetal mortality from voluntary or involuntary causes.

Mortality

Overview

In the present theory, mortality is differentiated from the rest of development (which is simply called "development"). This procedure is advisable and feasible in a longitudinal study of the Latin American region over the last forty to fifty years, since mortality decline and development have not been so intimately related as to preclude the possibility of separating their effects. There are two different mortality effects on natality—an immediate negative effect and a delayed positive one.

The Immediate Demographic Effect
of General Mortality Decline

There are many reasons for assuming that mortality decline has an initial natality-raising impact. A decrease in mortality generally raises the survival chances for married couples as child-producing units and thus promotes births (Arriaga, 1970b; Ridley et al., 1967). Furthermore, a decline in mortality is almost certainly associated with improvements in health, which in turn make it more probable that women will become pregnant and be able to carry a child to term (Davis and Blake, 1956; Freedman, 1963); this is *not* taken into account by the otherwise rather complete discussion of Ridley et al. (1967:78). Progress in health and nutrition also appear to lengthen the potential childbearing period of a woman's life (Tanner, 1965). Additional references on this topic are provided by Petersen (1969:173-80) and Ridley et al. (1967).

On the other hand, a decline in *infant* mortality may well lower the birth rate. This results partly from the fact that women who breastfeed their children are less susceptible to pregnancy (Jain et al., 1970; Ridley et al., 1967). Lower infant mortality also reduces motivation of replacing a lost child.

Theoretically, we would like to separate the immediate natality-decreasing effects of infant mortality decline from the opposite and more general effects of mortality decline and associated improvements in health and nutrition, but this is simply not feasible, due to the very poor measures of infant mortality in most Latin American countries. We may instead follow Arriaga (1970b) in assuming that the *net* immediate effect of a general mortality decline is to raise the birth rate. The magnitude of this effect will depend on factors such as the initial incidence of widowhood, norms governing remarriage, previous levels of health, fecundity, existing lactation practices, etc.

The Lagged Effect of Child
and Infant Survivorship

Statement of the assumption. There is a lagged and probably powerful effect of mortality decline which contributes to the long-term reduction of natality. This involves a process that is conceptually distinct from other aspects of socioeconomic development and from development-induced changes in societal values. Societies provide "protection" against high child and infant mortality through their belief systems. An increase in the survivorship rate of infants and children will, after a period of expanding family size, bring about a societal adjustment that will tend to reduce natality and bring the number of surviving children back nearer to its "old" level.

The notion of "insurance" births. It is conceivable that individuals in high mortality societies consciously realize that they are having extra births as "insurance." They might also consciously note an improvement in survival chances, and begin to use available methods of birth control to bring their natality more into line with their long-term desires. While this is possible, and no doubt occurs in some cases, the process is greatly oversimplified. It seems difficult for persons to recognize the decline of infant and child mortality, coming as it does rather gradually. It seems even more difficult for them to notice the disappearance of periodic but irregular and widely separated episodes of catastrophic mortality (e.g., famines, epidemics), which are an important component of child and infant survivorship. Furthermore, individuals in traditional societies or rural parts of developing societies have been known to express a desire for ten or more children, for "as many as God sends" or for "as many as possible" (Caldwell, 1967; Pool, 1970; Tabbarah, 1971). If individuals are acting on the basis of such desires, they have few if any "insurance" births to eliminate.

Many authors suggest that a conscious, rational "adjustment" to the new survivorship levels occurs. More recently this notion has been articulated by Wyon and Gordon (1971) and Abhayaratne and Jayewardene (1968:86). These formulations assume that the individual can make these subtle perceptions and rational calculations and translate them into action. This assumption is difficult to justify in the rather early stages of socioeconomic development, when the "adjustment" begins.

The alternative rationale for the long-term natality effect. In the long run, the adjustment to higher survivorship probably operates through a dilution of the values supporting parenthood. The very high premium placed on childbearing is partly attributable to high mortality itself. When a man says he wants fifteen children he may reflect a largely unconscious realization that one must seek to have a great many children in order to see even a few live to adulthood. In the present system, beliefs about survivorship are ascribed to society rather than to individuals. If a massive decrease in child and infant mortality does occur, many more couples will in fact have very large families. This in itself must reduce the status value of having many children because status value has some properties of a zero-sum game—in the economist's terminology, the increased supply lowers the price of the good. A man who already has twelve grandchildren may not be ecstatic about the birth of a thirteenth—more practically, he and his wife cannot be counted on for the contributions of time and wealth that could be made by less overworked grandparents. Furthermore, desiring fifteen children is one thing, but actually desiring a fifteenth when one already has fourteen is another. In these and many more subtle ways, increased survivorship slowly erodes the values that encourage childbearing at higher parities. Clearly this will not happen at once, but it must almost certainly happen in the long run.

A secondary effect of improvements in child survivorship. There is a second and more direct way in which higher survivorship can encourage natality adjustment. Inevitably the resulting population and family-size increase causes some obvious strains. Since mortality decline usually begins while a society is largely rural, one possibly serious problem may be a shortage of new land and/or the inability of existing farms to support larger families. There are also more subtle difficulties. Family structures appropriate for older high mortality conditions may be unable to handle the increase in numbers of surviving children and the expanding number of kin relationships of various types. Land tenure and inheritance practices that were adequate under high mortality may become inappropriate. (For a discussion of the demographic relevance of land tenure and inheritance systems in Europe, see Lorimer [1954:164-68].) The fact is not often recognized, but due to death and social and economic strains, household size in the major nonindustrial societies of the past was not typically large—it is thought to have been five or six in premodern China, below six in India, and generally under five in Egypt *circa* 1917 (Goode, 1964:44-45; Sjoberg, 1960:157-63). Even if persons in a given society profess to desire large families and households, the reality of a general increase in size may markedly intensify previous economic problems, and possibly socioemotional ones as well. The time necessary for lower mortality to cause significant strains depends greatly on the characteristics of the society in question.

The relationship between mortality decline and natality is rather complex. From the above discussion, however, one main assumption and one secondary assumption can be distilled.

Assumption 2: The immediate effect of mortality decline is to raise natality; the delayed effect of mortality decline is to reduce childbearing-parenthood values.

Assumption 3: A secondary effect of a decline in child and infant mortality is to increase the economic strains on families.

This theoretical system is made distinctive by pulling together some of the findings and speculations on mortality effects. Such assumptions as these may help explain both the gross anomalies of the European natality experience (e.g.,

England vs. France) and the fact that European natality declines often began as early in rural as in urban areas, or earlier (Carlsson, 1966). This theory asserts that under certain circumstances rural people can make a quick adjustment to improved survivorship, an event that generally occurs early in the development period (see Chapter 2).

Family Resources

Some explication is required to generalize the more quantifiable aspects of "strain" or its opposite, which will be called "resources" or "family resources." These resources are a fundamental determinant of natality. The norms of virtually all societies require that the head of a household provide for his family and that he have access to some kind of employment to do this. In agrarian societies, as already noted, the availability of arable land is a key factor in making family life possible. Other things being equal (e.g., development), scarcity of land encourages lower natality through either unconscious or conscious mechanisms, which may or may not include contraception and/or abortion (Slicher Van Bath, 1968; Friedlander, 1969; Easterlin, 1971).

In urban sectors of societies, the situation is not quite so clear. Here a job that will provide a "decent" income and acceptable security by current standards seems to fill the role of farmland in the rural areas. However, the availability of such employment is far more fluid than the supply of land, and the standards of "decency" are probably highly relative to expectations. Easterlin (1961, 1966) and Kirk and Nortman (1958; also Kirk, 1960) have utilized the assumption that expectations rise as levels of living rise, and that it is deviation from these expectations that causes the felt strain. This view is corroborated by a host of other investigators who also found a direct link between business cycles and natality (Hyrenius, 1946; Galbraith and Thomas, 1941; Silver, 1965; Basavarajappa, 1971; Hexter, 1925:9-37, 133-38; and others).

The availability and security of the means of family support relative to current normative standards is likely to have an independent effect on natality. Thus a society that values moderate-size families may actually have only small families during a serious economic downward turn. Rural people may be more likely to react in terms of delaying or avoiding marriage, while urbanites may depend more on contraception or abortion. Nevertheless, some rural people do use direct, self-conscious birth control, and some urban people do delay marriage without considering it as a form of birth control. The means of adjustment are not as important as the result.

Since access to agricultural land is important only for the traditional agrarian sector, the process of socioeconomic development gradually destroys the usefulness of "land availability" as a measure of economic well-being. As a society becomes developed, a measure based on short-term economic fluctuations (in monetary terms) becomes more meaningful. In developing societies, therefore, "family resources" embodies two distinct yet theoretically similar aspects. In either case better or improving economic conditions contribute to higher natality.

As presently conceptualized, "family resources" is not an exclusively economic factor, although it can easily be phrased in those terms. The practical availability of land obviously depends on kinship structure and the associated systems of land tenure and inheritance. For urbanites the all-important expectation levels are a function of norms about what one ought to be able to do for one's family. Clearly this variable involves a mixture of economic and sociological processes. The assumption follows.

Assumption 4: Natality is a direct function of the availability to those who normally have children of those resources defined as necessary for the responsibilities of family life; among the more modernized, urban sectors of society, resources must be measured against expectations that are themselves a function of established standards of living.

The process of development itself generates more resources and removes dependence on the relatively fixed supply of land. But development also raises standards of living, hence expectations, and in the long run this probably offsets the effects of expansion of resources available to families. Again the present theoretical scheme asserts that development can result in a temporary natality increase. This is gratifying in light of the positive relationship between income and natality which is occasionally observed (see Chapter 3). Some evidence for this relationship is given by Weintraub (1962) and Heer (1966).

Cultural Background

As part of the general strategy, this book attempts to avoid some problems of cultural relativity by concentrating on one broad cultural region, thus controlling in a rough way for some anticipated disturbances. The final assumption will be more explicit about the importance of cultural background (i.e., the peculiar characteristics of the indigenous, predevelopment culture) and its relevance for the natality transition. This will also allow an exploration of the relevance of cultural differences within the Latin American region.

A crucial factor facilitating development itself, as well as the changes in values and norms relating to natality and the implementation of birth control, appears to be "openness" or "predisposition" to modernizing influences. Some pre-existing cultures are more adaptable in this respect than others. A secondary consideration must then include the degree to which the culture was historically *exposed* to such influences. (In the developing world, "Westernizing" could almost be substituted for "modernizing.") In other words, the assumption must also take into account the degree of contact with *good* "role models" of development. The assumption then becomes:

Assumption 5: Natality decline is facilitated to the degree that a predevelopment culture is predisposed to modernizing influences and has the opportunity for contact with more developed societies. This effect operates by encouraging development and mortality decline, but there may be a direct effect upon natality as well.

Measurement is an obvious problem, since the assumption covers two distinct dimensions of culture: "predisposition" and "exposure." For various reasons, discussed below, Latin American countries can be grouped according to the criteria of assumption 5 without too much difficulty; however, the measurement problems inherent in the assumption could prove more troublesome if one tried to apply its ideas more generally, and it would then be advisable to measure predisposition and exposure separately.

The phrase in the assumption "is facilitated" is intended to imply that the presumed effect is nonadditive. In the long run, the impact of the preexisting culture and early cultural contacts should become less important. Therefore, this factor should explain the timing of events more directly than the levels of variables at any particular time. Greater openness and exposure to modernizing influences should predispose toward earlier sustained development, mortality decline, and natality decline.

Excluded Variables

*Probable Causal Position
and Importance*

There are many other potentially important determinants of natality with which the study will not be greatly concerned and which will not be operationalized in this research. Basically these fall into two categories: first, variables that could conceivably affect the posited causal system at many points. An example discussed below is religion. The second category more specifically impinges upon the implementation of birth control, for instance the presence of family planning programs and/or the practical availability of specific means of birth control. Some of the Davis-Blake (1965) "intermediate variables" also fall into this class, as would differences in sex roles and types of sexual unions that could influence the ease with which contraception or abortion can be used. The possible effects of excluding some of these factors from the operationalized model are briefly discussed.

Religion

Religion, especially Roman Catholicism, is often thought to have an independent effect on what the present causal model describes as "values," as well as on the moral and practical availability of birth control (Petersen, 1969:537-38; Kiser *et al.*, 1968:229-34; Westoff and Potvin, 1967:79-107, 215-18; Ryder and Westoff, 1971:67-86). The cross-societal significance of this factor, however may be exaggerated (Population Council, 1968). Furthermore, the actual behavior of persons in Latin America does not seem to be governed by the *doctrine* of the Roman Catholic Church, and one cannot assume that the relationship between doctrine and behavior is simple and direct.

Within the Latin American region there is no apparent relationship between a country's religiosity and its natality. Argentina, for example, is essentially a cultural extension of southern Europe, and the Catholic Church is strong there. Nevertheless, Argentina's birth rate is among the lowest in the region. Brazil, on the other hand, is a more cosmopolitan and secular society, but the birth rate is much higher there than in Argentina. In this case and in most others, socioeconomic development explains natality differentials that cannot be attributed to religion. Throughout the world, modernized Catholic countries (e.g., France and Italy) have low natality, while developing Catholic countries (e.g., the Philippines) have high natality. In this respect, Catholics do not seem fundamentally different from persons of other religious backgrounds.

Surveys in the Latin American region also support the view that catholicism is not a major obstacle to natality decline or even the use of contraception. In the early 1960s, the percentage of ever-married women in six major Latin American cities (Bogotá, Buenos Aires, Caracas, Mexico City, Rio de Janeiro, and San José) who expressed categorical disapproval of birth control varied from 2 percent to only 16 percent (Stycos, 1971:260-64). A survey of 331 lower-class women in Tegucigalpa, Honduras, soon after the 1968 papal encyclical banning all birth control except rhythm found no one who would admit that the doctrine would affect her behavior (Stycos, 1971:384) and 77 percent who expressed open disapproval of the Pope's position (Stycos, 1971:384). There are strong indications that Latin Americans are not prevented from limiting natality by catholicism; but the ultimate test for the present theoretical model is its ability to predict natality without considering the religious factor.

Family Planning Programs and the
Technology of Birth Control

Family planning programs are sometimes thought of as fundamental causes of natality decline. This study is not concerned with the evaluation of such programs, however. In the Latin American region during the period of interest (up to 1970), there simply were no really effective family planning programs. Therefore, the exclusion of this factor from the causal model cannot result in serious problems.

The technology of birth control could be more salient. It seems logical to assume that persons who can easily obtain good means of birth control will be more likely to limit natality at a given level of motivation than others who must use less desirable methods.

Quantifying the technology of birth control (as availale to persons in a given country) seems quite difficult. The actual technology is virtually a worldwide phenomenon, not confined to any one country. One must really try to get at the practical availability of various means of birth control. Measuring availability independent of the demand for birth control seems prohibitively difficult. Neither government pronouncements nor the laws regulating birth control, including abortion, give a very good indication of the extent to which birth control is actually available. The consumption of contraceptives, on the other hand, seems to measure use or demand more than availability.

This study must assume that, if the availability of given birth control methods is of overriding importance, then the other independent variables that *are* measured should not predict natality trends very well. Theoretically it is possible that it is development and mortality decline that give rise to a demand for birth control, which in turn causes an increase in the availability of preferred methods of birth control. I believe that this causal sequence is actually far closer to reality than the assumption that the mechanics of birth control determine natality. If development and mortality levels do predict natality very well, my view will be supported.

Those who strongly emphasize the importance of means of birth limitation generally ignore the obvious comparison of Europe and Latin America. In Europe, natality decline began long before modern means of contraception were widely known. Latin America, however, has maintained high natality in most places until very recently, despite the fact that much better means of contraception are available. If the means of birth control were the major cause of natality decline, one would have expected birth rates in Latin America to have fallen much sooner.

Sex Roles and Types of Sexual Unions

There are some major differences in sex roles and unions within Latin America. First, there is a contrast between nations influenced by southern Europe and the British and Dutch West Indies. Second, there are at least two subgroups within the former category. The countries influenced by southern Europe appear to have rather "chauvinist" conceptions of sex roles, as well as strong double standards of sexual behavior. However, an examination of natality patterns indicates that some of these populations begin childbearing rather early, while others do not. This suggests that some countries (notably those with stronger European ties) have social structures that regulate sexual behavior more effectively than others.

Unfortunately, it is very difficult to measure "family structure" in such a way as to establish a simple relationship with natality. Information on consensual unions indicates that this form of sexual relationship is prevalent in most of the tropical areas and is largely absent elsewhere, but the natality effect is unclear. Some consensual unions may be much less stable than actual marriages, and women may feel impelled to have children in an effort to make the relationship more permanent. Insofar as birth control demands the cooperation of both partners, natality decline is less likely when sexual unions are unstable and men are not strictly responsible for their offspring. Nevertheless, consensual unions may be less fertile because intercourse might be infrequent. Both Roberts (1957:297) and Stycos (1968:187-214) report lower natality in less stable unions in the West Indies. Neither are illegitimacy rates an unambiguous measure of the relevant aspects of family structure; illegitimacy has different meanings in different countries of the region.

To the extent that the above differences of family structure and sex roles affect natality and can be operationalized, they seem to be closely associated with the cultural factor already appearing in Assumption 5. The main distinctions are among the countries that are extensions of southern Europe, those influenced by southern Europe but composed mainly of Amerindians, and those in the Caribbean area that have had much broader outside contacts and have been peopled by blacks and East Indians.

When put together, the theoretical system can be sketched as shown in Figure 4-1.

Specific Hypotheses

Overview

We can now combine the basic assumptions with specific, empirical assumptions (antecedent condition statements) to derive hypotheses that can be operationalized. These hypotheses will be organized on three levels. First, we derive some predictions concerning the trends of natality decline in parts of Europe as compared with those in Latin America. The aim is to determine if essentially the same forces, illustrated by the theoretical model, could have been operating in both regions. Next, comparative longitudinal trends within Latin America are examined, using the longest possible series of data. We again seek to determine if the posited set of causal factors could account for the main features of the Latin

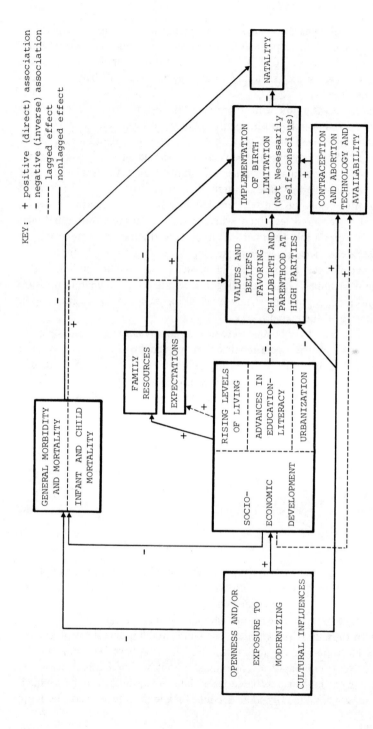

Figure 4-1. Causal Diagram of the Influences on Natality. Note: Probable reverse relationships are not shown; neither are possible weak links not directly affecting values, implementation, or natality. The assumptions add somewhat to the model illustrated by specifying more explicitly the nature of some relationships.

American experience. Finally, we focus on the postwar period, for which most data are available, and perform a pooled cross-sectional-longitudinal regression analysis seeking to achieve simultaneous control of the most relevant variables and to provide the most exacting test of the model.

Comparisons with Europe

In the long term, the model predicts that the course of socioeconomic change and mortality decline will determine natality trends (assumptions 1 and 2). Other factors in the model are either transitory or cyclical in their importance. Assumptions 1 and 2 can be combined with the hypothesis that mortality decline has proceeded much faster in Latin America than in northwestern Europe (Arriaga, 1970a), while development, at least in economic terms, seems to have gone forward at roughly the same pace (see Table 3-2). This implies that natality decline in Latin America, once begun, should generally be faster than historical natality declines in northwestern Europe. Note that the independent importance of the rapid Latin American mortality decline is a crucial assumption. Similar antecedent conditions lead to much the same conclusion regarding a comparison between Latin America and Italy. These hypotheses are not common in the literature, and their confirmation might be considered rather surprising. If we now compare Spain and Portugal to Latin America in terms of the pace of overall development and mortality decline, we would have to conclude that in Latin America natality decline should be *much faster* than in these Iberian countries. We therefore generate three subhypotheses:

Hypothesis 1a: Once begun, natality decline tends to proceed faster in Latin American societies than in comparable periods in northwestern Europe.

Hypothesis 1b: Once begun, natality decline tends to proceed faster in Latin American societies than in a comparable period in Italy.

Hypothesis 1c: Once begun, natality decline tends to proceed *much faster* (relative to comparisons with Italy and northwestern Europe) in Latin America than in comparable periods in Spain and Portugal.

It is impractical to attempt to derive a hypothesis comparing Latin America with eastern Europe. Historical data series for eastern Europe are complicated by the major effects of wars and numerous boundary changes. Both mortality decline and development seem to have proceeded rather rapidly in this area—certainly this would be the conclusion if judged by the experience of the Soviet Union (Kuczynski, 1931; Kuznets, 1964). Thus, the contrast with the Latin American experience is not so clear.

Explaining Differences across Latin
American Countries: Long-term Trends

Differences among countries of the Latin American region are now considered. Again it is assumed that eventually trends in mortality and development are dominant, and that other factors cause only transitory or minor disturbances in long-range natality trends. This is reasonable in view of previous observations (see especially Chapter 2 and the section on Japan in Chapter 3) of the dependability of long-term relationships predicted by transition theory. This leads to hypotheses analogous to 1a, 1b, and 1c, except that the independent variables (rates of mortality decline and development) appear in the hypotheses rather than in the antecedent assumptions.

Hypothesis 2a: Latin American countries that experience mortality decline at more rapid rates will have faster rates of natality decline.
Hypothesis 2b: Latin American countries that experience socioeconomic development at more rapid rates will have faster rates of natality decline.

It would also be desirable to explore the extent to which levels of development and mortality alone can identify those countries about to experience the onset of major natality decline. This is a risky procedure, however, since even the present theoretical model predicts that other variables can have substantial temporary effects that may hasten or retard the observed beginning of natality reduction. Therefore, the following hypothesis is presented with the provision that, to the extent exceptions can be explained by other variables in the model, they would not be regarded as refutations of the entire theory—although they would suggest that development and mortality alone are not as determinant of natality as might be anticipated.

Hypothesis 3: During a given period, those Latin American countries with lower mortality and higher levels of socioeconomic development will be more likely to experience the onset of major natality decline.

The phrase "during a given period" is injected to refrain from making this a "threshold" hypothesis. Instead, hypothesis 3 implies that the "threshold" levels (of mortality and development measures) associated with natality decline might be specific for historical periods even within the Latin American region.

The above hypotheses all depend on traditional transition theory ideas as stated in assumption 1 and the second portion of assumption 2. "Cultural background" is the only other causal factor in the present model that is thought to have a strong enough independent effect to be observed over the long term without controls on other variables. It is then necessary to define "cultural openness-exposure" so as to be measurable, and to determine exactly how natality should be affected by it.

Racial composition will act as the index of openness and exposure to modernizing influences. Within the Latin American region, racial composition is a fairly good indicator of the cultural background of a country. Furthermore, the racial classification seems to allow the conceptually distinct dimensions of "openness" and "exposure" to be combined for practical purposes of measurement.

Four types of Latin American countries are identified, proceeding in order from the most to the least open and exposed to modernizing influences. Countries of the region can then be ranked in several categories, along the resulting continuum. First there are countries that are very close to being European in both population and cultural tradition. Such countries are populated mainly by descendants of European immigrants; this represents the greatest openness and exposure to modernizing influences, which typically come from European societies. The second type of country either contains persons who have lost their indigenous culture (Africans, in this case) or has several minority groups in a culturally cosmopolitan setting. Countries close to this type are really the least "Latin" of the region, and are centered in the Caribbean. Racially they are distinguished by having few Europeans or Amerindians. A third type of Latin American country is mainly Amerindian in racial background, but also has some mixture of European ancestry. Typically those persons who are more obviously European form the upper classes in these nations. These may be called mestizo countries. The final type consists of an Amerindian population. Countries approximating this characteristic (overwhelmingly Amerindian) were in fact influenced by southern European societies, but never to the point of entirely losing their own culture. Furthermore, political control ended in the nineteenth century and these nations have been relatively isolated during the major period of European development. Thus, the continuum of openness and exposure to modernizing influences is assumed to run from European to African-East Indian to mestizo and finally to Amerindian populations.

Cultural "openness-exposure" should facilitate relatively early natality decline, mainly by allowing earlier socioeconomic development and mortality decline. The primary hypothesis by which the assumption is tested involves the total effect of cultural background upon the timing of major natality decline.

Hypothesis 4: The greater the openness and/or exposure to modernizing influences (measured racially as described above), the earlier the major natality decline of the demographic transition.

Secondarily, the analysis examines the effect of cultural background upon development and mortality trends, and also attempts to isolate any direct effect of culture upon natality (which is independent of development-mortality). The latter involves an examination of the variation in birth rates (not attributable to any other measured variable) in relation to culture. These residuals can be obtained from the regression analysis to be described below. If there is a systematic direct effect of culture, it should show up in the residuals, since other independent variables of the system are taken into account.

If there is a direct effect of culture, this factor would normally be included in the regression equation described below. This procedure is not followed here for several reasons. First, the effect of culture is assumed to be nonadditive and difficult to represent mathematically (this will be confirmed empirically in the following chapter). Second, this and other problems are aggravated by difficulties in quantifying culture. If *not* quantified, the cultural categories would have to be treated as dummy variables, and this would result in the use of many degrees of freedom that cannot be spared in an analysis that has only twenty-four cross-sectional units. Third, culture is assumed to operate principally through development and mortality so that we allow for most of its effect by having the latter variables in the equation. Finally, the impact of culture upon development and mortality is only of tangential interest in this study, and in view of the problems in measuring culture, it seems more reasonable to simply analyze the total effect of culture upon natality and make supplementary examination of the direct effects on natality. This is the strategy to be followed.

Relationships Among Variables with
Simultaneous Controls: Post World War II

The above hypotheses provide some test of the theoretical structure, but have the disadvantage of failing to control for other variables in the assumed causal system. In the regression analysis it is possible to apply such controls and to operationalize most components of the model. By using a combined longitudinal-cross-sectional approach it is also possible to correct certain other problems, including some that affect strictly cross-sectional regressions (see Chapter 5). Unfortunately, long-range trends cannot be examined due to the scarcity of good data before World War II.

The fundamental assumption 1 becomes:

Hypothesis 5: The direct, lagged effect of rising urbanization, education, and levels of living, as measures of development, is to reduce natality.

The above follows directly from the additional assumption that countries of the Latin American region are more or less in the hypothetical range of development to expect natality decline. This appears to be true generally, but may not apply to every case.

Assumption 2 requires two hypotheses:

Hypothesis 6: The immediate effect of general mortality decline is to raise natality.

Hypothesis 7: The direct, lagged effect of mortality decline, especially of infants and children, is to reduce natality.

When separated from associated immediate effects, the natality-reducing impact of mortality decline should be one of the most powerful determinants of natality, a statement that may be considered as an informal secondary hypothesis. The survivorship chances of children can greatly increase over the course of mortality decline, and a one-for-one adjustment of births could in itself account for much of the long-term natality decline. Practically speaking, however, it may be difficult to separate the effect of long-range changes in mortality from the development measures, because of their probable intercorrelation.

Assumption 3 is not operationalized because it entails no direct effect on natality. Rather it asserts that mortality decline can increase the strain on family resources, which in turn affects natality. This assumption was introduced for the sake of the completeness of the model. The regression analysis is greatly facilitated if attention is confined to direct relationships to natality, because the possible causal links among other variables in the system could become too complex to deal with.

Assumption 4 presents some serious measurement problems. Conceptually, family resources are all alike in some ways, but practically speaking, there is a peculiar dependence upon land in the traditional rural sector and upon wage-earnings-jobs in the more modern urban sector. Furthermore, there is the complicating factor of rising expectations in the latter. This dilemma is handled by again splitting the assumption into two hypotheses for purposes of operationalization.

Hypothesis 8: The direct effect of the availability of land resources upon natality, when weighted by the proportion of the population in the (traditional) rural sector, is positive.

Hypothesis 9: The direct effect of the rate of expansion of the money economy upon natality, when weighted by the proportion of the population in the (modern) urban sector, is positive.

These hypotheses avoid the problem of the changing "resource base" by developing two separate ideas. This is done to facilitate measurement. (A fuller discussion of the effects of the resource base is contained in the presentation of the results of the regression analysis in Chapter 7.)

Hypothesis 9 includes a crucial simplification that again facilitates measurement. It is assumed that expectations are strictly a function of past economic levels in each specific country. Although it ignores many subtleties, this assumption makes it possible to use growth rates as a measure of both economic level and expectations, and makes operationalization feasible.

Assumption 5 involves the idea of cultural background, especially openness and exposure to modernizing influences. It is not directly included in the regression equation, for reasons discussed in the derivation of hypothesis 4 above. The examination of the residuals of the regression analysis is intended to fulfill the function of testing assumption 5 insofar as direct effects are concerned.

It should be noted that the model does not attempt to examine all the possible relationships among the independent variables, or the possible reverse effects of natality upon them. The principal interest here is in the direct effects of the independent variables upon natality.

5 Methodology

Introduction

This study consists of a cross-sectional-longitudinal analysis of countries of the Latin American region (including Puerto Rico) with populations of over 500,000. "Latin America" is used as a synonym for the Latin American geographic region, even though not all of the countries included are culturally "Latin." The first part of the empirical analysis is a comparative assessment of long-term trends in light of the first four hypotheses. The second portion is a regression analysis, which takes as observations data for each Latin American country at five-year intervals during the post-World-War-II period.

This chapter moves from the general to the particular in discussing procedures and possible problems. The first section examines overriding methodological issues, with particular attention to those most likely to affect the present study. Next, difficulties encountered in using techniques other than regression to measure association are discussed. Means of evaluating each of the first four hypotheses are examined. We next consider the regression analysis, and focus on several problems of combined cross-sectional-longitudinal methods. Finally, there is a discussion and evaluation of the actual measures used in making the variables operational.

General Methodological Problems

The Ecological Fallacy

Findings obtained using aggregate units of analysis cannot be routinely generalized to individuals (Robinson, 1950). It can be shown that one can make a variety of fallacious inferences when data at one level of analysis are used to test a hypothesized relationship at another (Alker, 1969; Hannan, 1971). The present research operates exclusively at the macroscope level, and thus seeks to avoid these difficulties. Both hypotheses and data refer to national-level aggregations. It is of course true that a development measure, such as the percentage of the population that is urban, or even a natality measure such as the birth rate, can be considered an aggregation of individual characteristics; but each can also be thought of as a property of a social unit, since each is in fact a "rate" in the Durkheimian sense. It is not claimed that any of the hypotheses or modifications thereof are applicable to the individual or to groups within a given country. It would be fortunate if some of the findings would hold true at other levels, but that question is beyond the scope of the current investigation.

In practice we require a formal and unequivocal definition of the sample. The study uses areas south of the United States listed as separate entities in the United Nations *Demographic Yearbooks*, excluding those with populations under 500,000 in 1970. Except for Puerto Rico these are nation-stages. These Latin American countries seem to be emerging national societies in much the same sense as European nations were at one time. The theory of the demographic transition was really formulated with such social units in mind, and no serious difficulties should arise in using this sample.

Diffusion—Galton's Problem

Galton's problem is really a special case of nonindependence of observations. Since Latin American nations often share cultural backgrounds and are collectively influenced by outside forces, one could regard this area as one within which characteristics of countries may be associated merely because they were associated in some other area and have diffused together. The problem amounts to the following: Traits X and Y may occur together in social unit A; through contact with A, countries B, C, and D all adopt X and happen to adopt Y as well; in this case, there is really only one independent observation of a causal relationship between X and Y, that in unit A—the other instances are merely "reflections" of the first (Galton, 1889:272).

The diffusion problem is not particularly damaging to this investigation. Suppose that X is the set of independent variables, which in the long run is mainly socioeconomic development and mortality decline, and Y is the dependent variable, natality decline. The spread of X has surely been aided by diffusion and aided differentially so that contacts with appropriate Western models have probably hastened development in some countries more than others. This is the subject of hypothesis 4. At the same time, there is *not one* bona fide example anywhere in the world of a nation in which low natality (Y) was adopted without first achieving at least moderate development and mortality decline. Of course, one reason for this remarkable consistency is quite simple—lack of development has usually been associated with relatively high mortality, and it would be literally suicidal for any country to greatly reduce birth rates under these conditions. Thus, it does not seem likely that natality decline and its posited determinants can be associated simply because they have diffused together by chance.

The actual relationship may be described as "semi-diffusional" (Naroll, 1961:219-20): one in which traits tend to diffuse together *because* there is a functional (causal) relationship between them. This is essentially what the present model assumes. The causes of the independent variables, development and mortality decline, are not of concern here. The present theory states only that natality decline invariably follows after some lag. This should hold whether or not the technology of birth control is also diffused or is perfected independently; of course the completely independent invention of birth control methods is unlikely in present-day developing countries, to say the least. Relative to demographic transition theory, this provision implies that even if mortality decline and development are spread by diffusion, their long-range effect upon natality is unaltered, i.e., diffused changes in the independent variables are as meaningful as changes induced by local innovation. This idea is critical in the Latin American region, where it has been asserted that mortality decline (Arriaga, 1970b) and certain aspects of urbanization (Hauser, 1968) cannot be expected to have natality effects similar to those in Europe, because they have been induced by outside forces in some way.

Regional Study

Except for the hypothesis set 1, the empirical work is a regional study, in that comparisons are made only within Latin America. In cross-cultural research, this method has seldom been used to establish causal relationships, although demographers have often made *descriptive* regional studies. There are some rather formidable problems in doing causal analysis regionally (Naroll, 1968:242-44), including those stemming from diffusion, described above. Naroll (1968) points out that strong historical interdependence makes it difficult to establish causal connections on the basis of data from a single region. However, historical interdependence is not particularly problematic for the present study, for the same reason that diffusion is not very damaging: the hypothesized relationships are not likely to be present by historical accident. A major decline in the birth rate requires basic changes in norms and values. For this reason, it is very probable that an empirical confirmation of the theory is due to the existence of the posited causal relationships. It must be admitted, however, that historical interdependence, like diffusion, implies that each unit of the sample is not strictly independent of every other.

It is nonetheless possible that because of some peculiar antecedent condition, causal relationships established in one region may not be generalizable to another. This is a valid criticism, but it should be noted that the theory of the demographic transition was originally formulated on the basis of European experience and has been attacked as being somehow specific to that area. The present study tests the applicability of transition theory to one more cultural region.

Means of Assessing Association of
Variables Other Than Regression Analysis

Overview

The first several hypotheses involve comparisons of rates of natality decline (1a, 1b, 1c) and their relation to other variables (2a, 2b). It is also necessary to establish an association between the levels of socioeconomic and mortality indicators and the occurrence of natality decline (3). Finally, we must assess the relationship between cultural categories and the timing of natality decline as well as the residuals of natality from the regression analysis (4).

Hypotheses 1a-1c

Hypotheses 1a, 1b, and 1c simply require comparing rates of natality decline. The specific method for measuring these rates will be set forth in the next chapter; however, the measure will be based on country data and the hypotheses call for European and Latin American regional comparisons. Summary regional statistics will be determined from the country rates by calculating medians, means, and means weighted by population. Note that these hypotheses examine only those Latin American countries that have been experiencing natality decline for several years—only these have natality decline rates to measure. If the rest of the theoretical structure is verified however, there will be no reason to expect other Latin American countries to behave differently if and when their natality declines begin.

Hypotheses 2a and 2b

Hypotheses 2a and 2b require the comparison of rates of natality decline with rates of change in development and mortality indicators. Once measures of rates of change in development and mortality have been determined (Chapter 6), these will be correlated with rates of natality decline. Either rank-order or product-moment correlations might be appropriate, depending on the measures.

Due to the small sample size (again, only countries with natality declines qualify) zero-order correlations will be used. The combined effect of the predictor variables, if much different from individual effects, will have to be assessed by ascertaining whether cases that prove to be exceptions according to one independent variable can be explained by others.

Hypothesis 3

Hypothesis 3 attempts to assess the reliability with which levels of mortality and development measures could have identified those countries most likely to begin a major natality decline in the immediately ensuing period. It will first be necessary to determine the approximate times at which Latin American natality declines have begun. We can hope that these dates will cluster into a small number of short periods. If so, the immediately previous development and mortality levels of all Latin American countries (that had not already experienced major natality decline) will be listed. Coefficients of separation (the percentage of possible paired comparisons for which an independent variable makes an accurate prediction) will then be calculated to ascertain how well these independent variables would have differentiated the countries about to have natality declines from those whose natality was to remain high.

Again, each coefficient of separation involves only one predictor. The combined effect of independent variables, if much different from the individual effects, must be assessed by a consideration of cases that are anomalous for one variable but might be explained by others.

Hypothesis 4

This hypothesis states that an aspect of cultural background called "openness and exposure to modernizing influences" affects the timing of natality decline. Secondarily, we wish to determine if the cultural factor is related to unexplained residuals of natality. Since cultural openness-exposure will be measured categorically (see pp. 56-58), these ideas can be tested by ascertaining whether the predicted progression in time of onset of natality decline and natality residuals across cultural categories appears.

Problems and Advantages of the Regression Analysis

General Description

A multivariate regression of natality on most of the independent variables of the theoretical system will evaluate hypotheses 5-9. Unlike the several other studies that have used regression to assess sociodemographic theory in Latin America, this will be longitudinal as well as cross-sectional. Each country at a given time will be treated as a separate observation. To enhance reliability of annual data and to avoid the problem of unavailability of certain measures at more frequent intervals, observations will be for five-year periods. Due to restrictions of data, only the post-World-War-II period will be included. This results in an N of 96 (four observations on each of twenty-four countries).

Consideration is now given to some specific methodological issues raised by such analysis. The general form of the regression equation is:

$$\text{Natality}\,(t) = b_0 + b_1 \text{ urbanization}\,(t-1) + b_2 \text{ education}\,(t-1)$$
$$+ b_3 \text{ levels of living}\,(t-1) + b_4 \text{ mortality}\,(t)$$
$$+ b_5 \text{ mortality}\,(t-1) + b_6 \text{ weighted land resources}\,(t)$$
$$+ b_7 \text{ weighted economic expansion}\,(t, t-1)$$

where t designates present time, $t-1$ some prior time, and the b's are regression coefficients; economic expansion is a rate of change that depends on absolute levels of an economic variable at both the present and past time.

Linearity

The hypotheses refer to monotonic relationships while the regression model tests for linear relationships, a special case of the former and hence a more demanding requirement which could result in "Type I" error, mistaken refutation (Labovitz, 1970).

These problems will be dealt with on a measure-by-measure basis by looking for any indication that a given measure could be related to natality in a monotonic but nonlinear manner. Various transformations of the independent variables will be tried in order to "linearize" possible nonlinear relationships.

Reverse Causation

It is conceivable that a negative association between the lagged development-mortality variables and natality could be partly due to a retarding effect of high birth rates on social change and economic progress. There may be other reasons to suspect that natality could affect the nonlagged independent variables and also distort findings relevant to them.

For the lagged independent variables, there are two separate ways of dealing with the reverse causation problem: analysis of changes over time and direct argument on the basis of observed long-term trends. The longitudinal aspect of the present study allows development and mortality at time t to be related to the *change* in natality over the following period. This eliminates reverse causation by making the relevant natality changes subsequent in time to the independent variables. Following the suggestion of Bohrnstedt (1969), changes in natality are measured by the part of natality at the later time not attributable to natality at an earlier time. Thus natality at the earlier time becomes a predictor in the regression equation and the other (the "real") independent variables must explain the deviations in later natality not predicted by its earlier value. This measure of change has been shown to be statistically superior to the usual "change score," which is simply the arithmetical difference of two values (Bohrnstedt, 1969).

A direct argument can also be made to defend the assertion that reverse causation cannot be a major problem insofar as the lagged independent variables are concerned. Usually reverse causation is thought of as working through a retarding impact of high natality on development (and/or mortality decline). However, in Latin America since World War II, very rapid socioeconomic progress and mortality decline has coexisted with high natality and rapid population growth. Thus, *in this region and at this time* the retarding effect cannot have been great enough to cause serious problems. It can also be argued that, in Latin America since 1950, significant development and mortality decline have *always* preceded natality decline, but the reverse has never happened. This strongly suggests that causation moves mainly from the lagged development and mortality measures to natality, rather than vice versa. (This argument is similar to that developed more fully on pp. 62-63).

The nonlagged independent variables are assumed to affect contemporaneous natality, and the deviations of natality over time used to eliminate reverse causation with the lagged independent variables may not be effective. The nonlagged variables therefore require individual consideration for the possible biasing effects of reverse causation.

The availability of farm land may be reduced by persistent high natality, but this is a negative relationship (high natality, low availability), whereas the predicted association is positive (high availability, high natality) so that the bias is conservative. In any case, only natality in the last five years must be considered, since we can control for natality five years previous to each observation; it is doubtful that natality changes over five years will markedly affect the availability of land.

The impact of general mortality on contemporaneous natality is potentially more troublesome. High natality and low mortality may both result from a young age structure, and this is a negative relationship, exactly as predicted in hypothesis 6. Partly, this problem is obviated by the control for natality five years previously; typically, the overall age structure will not change markedly in five years. Second, one of the two natality measures is standardized for age structure. Both of these mitigating factors serve to control for the spurious relationship acting through age structure. So long as the age-standardized and crude birth rates give similar findings, this bias can probably be discounted.

Finally, recent natality could conceivably affect economic expansion measured by growth in real national product over five years. Measurement in absolute rather than per capita terms does invite the observation that population growth contributed to total output, which would spuriously support the hypothesized positive relationship between natality and economic expansion. However, the control for natality five years previous to the observation again means that only recent natality trends are crucial. It is doubtful that anyone under five years of age will make much of a contribution to economic production. It may be that his parents or someone else works harder to support him, but this is a psychological factor, scarcely measurable. The logical alternative measure of economic expansion, one based on per capita measures, would have much more serious problems of reverse causation, since population growth (closely related to natality) during the last five years would actually be built into the denominators of the economic measures.

Multicollinearity

This is a persistent problem for quantitative sociodemographic research. When independent variables are highly intercorrelated, it becomes very difficult to attribute causation to one or the other with confidence (Wonnacott and Wonnacott, 1970:257-59).

Multicollinearity must be anticipated among the five mortality and development variables in the study. The peculiarities of Latin America reduce these problems somewhat. Although mortality is related to development, there are causal considerations which suggest that this relationship is not so close as to prove an insurmountable problem. The present availability of effective public health programs and the increasing desire of governments to use them allows for a greater independence of mortality from socioeconomic development than was possible in Europe. (I will continually stress, however, that this independence is far less than sometimes imagined.)

Correlation between present general mortality and lagged child and infant mortality is bound to be very high, and may make the separation of effects required by hypotheses 6 and 7 impossible. This problem will be borne in mind when constructing measures of mortality. Since the hypothesized effects of the two aspects of mortality are opposite, however, it seems unlikely that the predicted result would come about by chance.

No formal hypotheses about the particular effects of various aspects of development have been made. For this reason, their intercorrelation is not a serious theoretical problem. Nevertheless, the degree of their interdependence may not be so great (see Chapter 7) as to preclude a consideration of their possible separate effects.

For the family resources variables (land availability and economic expansion), multicollinearity is not a critical impediment. Measuring economic expansion by growth of absolute national produce should keep the correlation with per capita national product (a development measure) low. The other potential source of damaging multicollinearity results from the inclusion of urbanization (a development measure) in the "weighting" factors of economic expansion and land availability—each is weighted by the proportion of the population in the urban or rural sector, respectively. This objection is best answered by an examination of the actual correlations between the family resources measures and urbanization (Chapter 7), which we can hope will not be too high.

Tests of Significance

Significance tests are not very meaningful in this type of longitudinal analysis. Strictly speaking, such tests require an assumption of independence of observations which cannot even be approximated with repeated observations on the same unit. In addition to significance tests, the strength of relationships will be assessed in light of unstandardized regression coefficients. These coefficients will be used to estimate the change in natality to be expected as a result of the changes in each independent variable likely to occur during the main portion of socioeconomic development; the more natality change expected, the stronger the presumed relationship. This seems to be more informative than significance tests, because other regression studies have sometimes yielded coefficients that, though "significant," would make absolutely no sense if projected over the likely *historical* experience of a developing country (Janowitz, 1971).

Despite their present inappropriateness, significance tests do have some appeal in that they are generally accepted measures of the reliability of results. For this reason, significance tests will be calculated with two alternative assumptions: (1) that the N is the total number of observations (usually 96), and (2) that the N is the number of units (24). Although these tests should provide some rough idea of "true" statistical significance, they will be presented only as a matter of information, and no assertion as to their validity is made.

Correlation of Errors

This is the bane of time-series regression. The standard regression model involves the assumption that the unexplained residuals of natality be independent of each other. If some other variable, not explicitly in the equation, affects a country's natality at a certain time and again in the next period, those two observations will have correlated residuals (autocorrelations). Fortunately, regression coefficients (unstandardized) remain unbiased even with autocorrelation, and the main problem created is the decrease of effective sample size. This has the effect of disturbing significance tests, which is not crucial to this study, but also tends to increase the sampling variance of the regression coefficients, which is more problematic (Johnston, 1972:246).

An attempt to utilize known techniques that can sometimes correct for autocorrelation will be initiated after performing ordinary least-squares regression. To do this most easily, it is necessary to assume that the serial dependence of the error terms is a linear first-order Markov process, so that the error at time t depends on previous errors *only* through the effects of the error at the immediately previous period. This assumption may or may not be valid, but can sometimes be tested. With this assumption, the Durbin-Watson statistic provides a test for the hypothesis of no autocorrelation (Wonnacott and Wonnacott, 1970:142-43). Unfortunately, this test is not at all reliable for short times series such as those used in the present study.

An alternative is simply to estimate the dependence from the observed autocorrelation of the error term. This is likely to be an underestimate of the true autocorrelation (Wonnacott and Wonnacott, 1970:144), but nonetheless provides important information. After estimation of the autocorrelation there are three possibilities. If the estimated value of the dependence term is near 1, autocorrelation might be purged with the technique of first differences, but the validity of the resulting estimates is questionable (Wonnacott and Wonnacott, 1970:143). If the result is moderate autocorrelation, the observed dependence term may be used as an estimate of the true value and the regression redone substituting "corrected" data, which would have the form $X^*(t) = X(t) - rX(t-1)$. $X^*(t)$ is the corrected value at time t, $X(t)$ is the original value at time t, $X(t-1)$ is the original value at the previous period, and r is the estimate of the linear dependence (autocorrelation) (Wonnacott and Wonnacott, 1970:330). Finally, if the estimated dependence term is near zero, little or no autocorrelation is indicated and no correction of the data is necessary.

Autocorrelation cannot be readily corrected, however, unless the assumption of a first-order Markov dependence relationship is allowed. In this analysis, such an assumption can be tested because there are twenty-four different units observed over time. The assumption requires that the partial correlation of a residual (error) at period $t+2$ with its value at t be close to zero when the residual at the intervening period, $t+1$, is controlled. If true, there is reason to believe that the residual at $t+2$ is affected by the residual at t only through the intervening residual, $t+1$. If some such simplification is not defensible, there is no widely accepted technique for purging autocorrelation, and the increased sampling variance of the regression coefficients must simply be tolerated.

Lag Times

The theory calls for lagged effects of the development and one of the mortality measures on values, and hence on the birth rate. Unfortunately, the lengths of these lags i not specified, nor is it known that only one lag is involved. The regression model requires knowledge of the exact length and complexity of the lag. In fact the lags are probably far longer than any measured with post-World-War-II data. The causal lags may very possibly be as long as fifteen years to a generation. If the true lags are long and if the indicator tends to change monotonically, as we believe, then the closer the data approach the actual lag the better, and even a very short lag is better than none. With the data set to be used, mortality can be lagged ten years. Urbanization, levels of living, and education can be lagged about seven and one-half years (e.g., urbanization in

1950 would be a predictor of natality in 1955-60). For the first period of the analysis, predicting natality 1950-55, shorter lags will be necessary for some variables, ranging down to three years, depending on the country and the indicator. Some experimentation with longer lags (which means a reduction in the number of observations) will be attempted to ascertain possible effects on causal implications.

Summary

Obviously, there are many problems associated with this type of research, partly because it is longitudinal and partly because it is theoretical. The extra effort of longitudinal analysis is justified because cross-sectional regression cannot do certain things, and in any case has already done much of what it is capable of accomplishing. The attempt at operationalization of a theory forces us to construct measures rather than opportunistically using any available, but should provide more meaningful results in the end.

Measurement

In this section we consider means of measuring variables and rates of change in variables. Multiple measures are proposed, because the long-term comparative analysis and the shorter-term regression study have different advantages and drawbacks, including the ability to handle certain defects in data. Also, better measures of some variables are available for the shorter period of observation.

The variables and measures to be used are as follows.

Natality:	Crude birth rate, age-sex standardized birth rate, gross reproduction rate.
Mortality:	Crude death rate, expectation of life at birth.
Socioeconomic development:	*Urbanization*—Percentage of the population defined as urban, percentage of the population in cities of 50,000 and 100,000 or more.
	Education—Literacy rate, percentage of the relevant age group in primary or secondary school, proportion of the total population in primary or secondary school.
	Levels of living—Net domestic product per capita in 1963 dollars of the United States, gross national product per capita, telephones per 100,000 population.

Land resources (land
  availability):   Total land area per 1000 rural population trans-
                                  formed logarithmically and weighted by the per-
                                  centage of the population that is rural.

Resources in the money
  economy corrected by
  expectations (economic
  expansion):   The rate of change in the absolute gross domestic
                                  product over the last five years (in real terms).

Cultural background: Approximate racial composition of the population
                                  (categorical measure).

Natality

The most widely available measure is the crude birth rate (CBR), the number of births per thousand population. This measure can be greatly affected by age structure and by factors that distort age structure, such as migration. Nevertheless, most distortions of this type tend to be reduced in the long run, so the crude birth rate may be quite acceptable for the first part of the analysis. The real difficulties come from registration omissions. These lead to lower reported rates for less-developed societies. Furthermore, registration typically improves over time, so true declines may be obliterated and spurious increases may be reported. The United Nations makes some assessment of registration completeness, but this does not extend to the more remote past, and the UN sometimes tends to a liberal view of the accuracy of statistics. Currently, many Latin American countries have reasonably good registration systems, but very few have reliable series going far back. For historical data one cannot rely on uncorrected official data in most cases.

Collver (1965) has attempted to estimate birth rates for most Latin American countries and to correct for underregistration. He usually presents both crude birth rates and the age-sex standardized birth rate, which is probably preferable. Actually, this "standardized" rate is really indirectly standardized on the assumption of a fixed set of proportions among age-specific natality levels. The most obvious error of this method stems from its assumption that age-specific natality for ages fifteen to twenty is only one-seventh that for ages twenty to twenty-five. In many Latin American societies, teenage natality is much higher than indicated by this ratio. Nevertheless, it is realistic in some cases and, since one must make some kind of assumption that does not fit every case, this indirect standardization is probably as good as any.

More important is the probable accuracy of Collver's corrections for underregistration. His technique is based on an attempt to make census materials, birth and death rates, and migration data consistent, using whatever information is available. Unfortunately, primary data, especially *good* primary data, are scarce in some cases, especially in the more distant past and the less-developed areas. In dealing with such problems, Collver often resorts to ad hoc assumptions which, while seldom unreasonable, are often arbitrary. In considering the possibilities for more systematic error, one might point out that infants who die a few months or even a few years after birth (often a large number) could be missed entirely. Their births may not have been registered, and registration of deaths is usually even less complete for infants than for older persons. Furthermore, these infants will probably not be recorded in any census. These omissions systematically bias recorded birth rates downward for countries with poor data compared with those ascribed to countries with more complete registration. Also, registration tends to improve while infant death rates fall, so that the bias is not constant but declines over time. Thus even Collver's data could obscure natality declines and/or build in spurious rises. Nevertheless, these data are normally better than official statistics, and are more appropriate for the purpose at hand.

In an effort to provide some information as to the nature of the biases in Collver's method, I reexamined post-World-War-II birth rates in two nations where he found natality increases—Costa Rica and Mexico. An alternative method, reverse survival, was used. Estimates based on this procedure also obtained a natality rise, but of smaller magnitude than Collver's data. The actual differences between the reverse survival estimates and those of Collver were quite small, however, and certainly not enough to throw great suspicion on his results.

The primary source of natality data before World War II that cannot be taken from reliable official sources will therefore be Collver (1965). Crude rates will be freely used for the analysis of long-term trends.

The regression study will use estimates of crude rates taken from United Nations sources (United Nations, 1969: United Nations, *1970 Demographic Yearbook*). By concentrating on the post-1950 period, these estimates can make use of better raw data than Collver, and have the advantage of including every nation of the present sample (whereas Collver excludes some). These crude rates will be standardized indirectly, using the same method employed by Collver (1965), with estimated age distributions of female populations from fifteen to forty-five taken from CELADE (1968).

Refined measures of natality are not widely available for Latin American countries. Where such data can be found it is typically in the official publications of the handful of countries with good vital statistics. These data are usually reproduced in the United Nations *Demographic Yearbook*s. Especially for the longer-range study, supplementary analyses will be made, where possible, using more refined (directly standardized) natality measures such as gross reproduction rates.

Mortality

Measuring this variable in the long term is comparatively easy, since one can use the results of censuses even if carried out at irregular intervals. Furthermore, Arriaga (1968) has made a monumental effort to produce life tables for Latin America, going back as far as possible. These provide an excellent and commonly accepted mortality measure, the expectation of life at birth, which will be used for the long-term analysis where available.

Again, there are some problems with Arriaga's estimation techniques, mainly with estimating infant mortality. To the extent that the errors are similar across nations and time periods, they cause few problems, since the present study requires only comparative measures of mortality and rate of mortality decline.

As an alternative mortality measure, crude death rates calculated by Collver (1965) will also be used. These are subject to problems similar to his estimates of crude birth rates. Crude death rates are also available from some other countries, excluded by Collver, which have had reasonably complete death registration; most of these are in the Caribbean, and their data are collected in United Nations *Demographic Yearbooks*.

For the post-World-War-II regression analysis, estimates of both crude death rates and expectation of life are available from the United Nations (1969). Although these estimates certainly are not perfect, they have the advantage of concentrating on the more recent period, when primary data are more readily available, and of being calculated on the basis of uniform procedures.

Hypotheses 6 and 7 require a measure of general mortality and a separate measure of child-infant mortality. These goals can only be approximated. The crude death rate (CDR) is the only widely available index of general mortality. The CDR counts the death of each individual equally, regardless of age. In contrast, the expectation of life at birth is (e_0), proposed as an indicator of child-infant survivorship (the complement of mortality) because it gives greater weight to the deaths of the young, who lose many more years of potential life. Ideally we would prefer a direct measure of child-infant mortality, but these statistics are often among the poorest of all demographic data. Furthermore, under the usual assumptions by which life tables are calculated from incomplete data, there is a perfect or near-perfect correlation between child-infant survivorship and e_0. Problems of inference resulting from correlation between the CDR and lagged e_0 and the age-structure dependence of the CDR were considered previously in this chapter, and we will remain alert to possible difficulties when the empirical results are examined.

Socioeconomic Development

Socioeconomic development will be measured mainly in terms of three basic subcomponents: urbanization, education, and levels of living. Each of these is substantively interesting in its own right, and certainly more than a mere index. Each will be measured seven and one-half years previous to birth rates, to allow for the assumed lag effect.

Urbanization will be measured primarily by the percentage of the population said to be "urban." This will be the only measure of urbanization in the regression analysis, and will also play an important role in the long-term study. Although there is considerable variance across nations in the definition of "urban," Davis (1969:18) concludes that the official data are often quite comparable from one place to the next. Fortunately, estimates of the percentage "urban" that attempt to improve on official data are available since 1950 (Davis, 1969; United Nations, 1970). The latter series will be used for the regression analysis, since it includes observations every five years as opposed to every ten years in Davis (1969). Before 1950, official data must be relied upon more heavily. However, where the later data show marked discrepancies with independent estimates, an effort will be made to "correct," at least in some approximate way, earlier statistics.

For the long-term analysis, information on the proportion of the population in cities of 50,000 and 100,000 or more is also available from Banks (1971) and the United Nations *Demographic Yearbook* respectively. These measures have the great advantage of seeming more objectively defined than "percentage urban," and also require data on only a few cities and total population. Unfortunately, the number of such cities is not constant and, especially in a small country, the measures can jump erratically when a new city reaches the 50,000 or 100,000 mark. Furthermore, they can be affected by vagaries in the definition of cities, suburbs, and metropolitan areas. Nevertheless, these measures should prove useful supplements to other data, and have the great advantage of being widely available back to the 1910-20 period for many countries.

Adult literacy and proportion of the children in school will be used as measures of essentially the same aspect of social change, even though literacy changes are slower, due to the older illiterates in a population. In the long-term analysis, both types of data will be used, but the school enrollment data can only be obtained in terms of the proportion of the total population in school (Banks, 1971). This indicator can be distorted by age structure in much the same way as crude birth and death rates, but probably is a reasonably good index in the long run. Fortunately, literacy data can also be found for a number of countries, and is typically collected in the United Nations *Demographic Yearbook*s.

For the regression analysis, only school enrollment data are available for enough countries at regular intervals. (Literacy data requires censuses, which unfortunately have not been carried out regularly in many places.) Since World War II, enrollment in primary or secondary schools as a proportion of those five to nineteen years of age can be found from United Nations sources (UNESCO, *Statistical Yearbook*s). Although this measure can sometimes be distorted by adult education programs and differences in the number of years of education required by a school system, these problems are less crucial *within* the Latin American region. For 1965 only, the United Nations has calculated "adjusted" school enrollment ratios which attempt to correct for some of these problems. For the twenty-four countries in the present sample, the correlation between the "raw" and "adjusted" combined primary-secondary ratios was .966. This suggests that it is reasonably safe to use the unadjusted rates for the post-World-War-II period.

Finally, a measure of levels of living is required. Information on various measures of national product per capita will be used for this purpose. It would be far better to be able to make some correction for income distribution, but this is not feasible, especially since information on time trends would also be needed. As it stands, some might wish to regard national product exclusively as a measure of production. While I feel that it is still an adequate surrogate for levels of living, the alternative interpretation is also tenable. In any case, national product per capita should still be an indicator of socioeconomic development.

Other criticisms are commonly directed to measures of national product, but none seem critical for the present purpose. It is probable that underdeveloped countries, not having an extensive money economy, have apparent national products below the actual (theoretical) levels (Morgenstern, 1963:277-78). This does not damage the usefulness of the measure as a comparative index of development, but only accentuates the split between "richer" and "poorer" countries.

Long-term data on national product are rather scarce. Very selective historical information on gross national product per capita is available from the World Bank (International Bank, 1970). In fact, data on long-term trends in most countries are nonexistent. A rough idea of early levels of national product can be obtained from more recent data, if one is willing to assume that national product per capita rarely declines in the long run.

For the post-World-War-II regression analysis, estimates of gross domestic product at factor cost in 1963 United States dollars can be obtained. The United Nations provides especially good and complete estimates for the year 1963 (*Statistical Yearbooks*). These have been extended forward and backward in time on the basis of series of index numbers of real per capita product also provided by the United Nations (*Statistical Yearbooks*) as well as the World Bank (International Bank, 1970). In a few cases, it may be necessary to use the change in some other indicator of national product as a guide in estimating the trend in gross domestic product.

Family Resources: Land Availability
and Economic Expansion

These variables are posited as lesser determinants of natality than socioeconomic development and (long-term) mortality. Hence, their effects would be difficult to observe without controls on these other independent variables. Since such controls can be applied only via multivariate analysis (or an extremely large sample), land availability and economic expansion are analyzed only in the regression study.

For rural persons, the primary resource is assumed to be usable land. This will be measured in terms of the natural logarithm (*ln*) of total land area per thousand rural population, i.e., *ln*(land area/rural population in 1000s). Arable land would appear to be more appropriate, but often represents land actually cultivated rather than potentially usable. The term is also inconsistent, in that grazing land and pasture is sometimes included, but not always. The natural log transform is applied to reflect the assumption that differences in land supply are more important when land is scarce, and become less so as it becomes plentiful. The relevant data on land appear in the United Nations *Statistical Yearbooks*, and estimates of rural population can be found in a special series prepared by the United Nations (1970). Finally, since it is assumed that land loses its importance as a direct resource for most of the population as development (and urbanization) proceeds, land supply is weighted by the proportion of the population that is rural.

For the urban population, resources relative to expectations are measured by rate of expansion of net domestic product over the previous five years. Again, this is weighted by the percentage of the population that is urban, both in order to account for numerical contribution of urbanites to the birth rate and to reflect the fact that with development, the money economy takes on greater importance. There is of course an implicit assumption that expectations depend on the economic situation about five years ago—not an unreasonable assumption, and the only practical one that can be operationalized with the data at hand; any longer-range expectation base would make it impossible to obtain information for some periods. Total rather than per capita product is used in order to measure the extent to which the country can *potentially* absorb new entrants, rather than the extent to which population increase is diluting gains in national product.

Cultural Background

The degree to which a country's cultural background has been open and exposed to modernizing influences has already been partially defined as a progression from European to "African" to "mestizo" to Amerindian. The only reasonably objective measure of position along this hypothetical continuum is based on racial composition. Race serves as a surrogate for cultural characteristics and experiences, not, needless to say, as a biological factor. There is no really comparative quantitative data on racial composition for many countries of the region; however, Preston James (1969) provides impressionistic and graphic information for every country. The *Statesman's Yearbooks* also give racial information, and indicate principal language groups from which approximate racial composition sometimes can be inferred. Also, a few countries include racial questions in their censuses, but the categories (e.g., "white") are not always comparable. Together, these sources can be used to construct a series of categories that can be placed along the hypothesized continuum.

Rates of Change

The first part of this research calls for measuring rates of change in mortality, natality, and development indicators. For birth rates, this can be accomplished by fitting a curve to the period of continuous decline, and using the resulting regression coefficient (and indication of slope) as a rate of decline. Of course this is justified only if a single type of curve fits all birth rate series reasonably well, and if periods of natality decline can be isolated. Experience suggests that such a curve can be obtained, and that, in fact, a straight line works remarkably well (see Chapter 6). The period of natality decline is usually easy to define, although there are problematic cases (e.g., Chile).

Another way of measuring rates of change is to observe the number of years required to move between two "benchmark" levels of the variable in question. Unfortunately, it is sometimes difficult to find benchmark levels of mortality or development indicators that can be observed in all or most countries of the relevant sample. This technique will be used where possible.

Finally, change scores (the absolute or percentage changes per time period in a variable) are an obvious way to measure rates of change. Although such measures have been shown to possess undesirable statistical properties (Bohrn-stedt, 1969), they do have intuitive appeal, and more important, can be calculated even on the basis of infrequent observations and used with small samples. Change scores will be used when better measures cannot be obtained.

Onset of Natality Decline

Testing the hypotheses requires an objective determination of whether or not a particular country has begun to have a major natality decline, and if so, the time at which natality started to drop. A country will be judged to have or have had declining natality if the crude birth rate has fallen 15 percent or more from its maximum three- or five-year average, and has moved below 35 without subsequent reversals. The combination of these criteria eliminates countries fluctuating widely at high levels. The exact procedures are presented in the next chapter. The onset of natality decline will be taken as the mid-year of the maximum immediately preceding a natality decline of 15 percent or more. Obviously, this need not be a good measure of the year of onset of natality decline. It is objective, however, and for the present body of data the measure seems to give good results. That is, when the dates of the beginning of natality decline are determined in this way (see Chapter 6), the answers are very similar to those obtained by close examination of each series on a case-by-case basis.

6

Long-Term Sociodemographic Trends (Hypotheses 1-4)

Hypotheses 1a, 1b, and 1c

Procedures

Determination of the sample. These hypotheses state that natality declines in Latin American countries should be more rapid than those of northwestern Europe or Italy, and much more rapid than those of the Iberian countries. In order to make the required comparisons of rates of natality decline, it is first necessary to identify those nations that have experienced or are experiencing natality declines in the relevant areas of northwestern Europe and Latin America.

All the nations that could conceivably be considered in "northwestern Europe" have experienced major natality declines, so that only the problem of geographic definition remains; however, there is an additional complication in that national boundaries changed during the period of interest. It was found that data collection was facilitated by using the national units listed by Kuczynski (1928) for *circa* 1875. Belgium, Denmark, England and Wales, France, Germany,[a] Ireland, the Netherlands, Norway, Scotland, Sweden, and Switzerland are included. Austria and Finland are marginal cases that could also have been added; however, their inclusion would have had little effect on the findings.

Within the Latin American region as defined in Chapter 5, it is sometimes difficult to ascertain which countries are experiencing the major natality decline of the demographic transition. Operationally, a nation that has lowered the CBR by 15 percent or more from its three-year peak (five-year if lacking annual data) to a level of 35 or less was defined as having begun natality reduction. The eight nations that attain this criterion appear without a "b" footnote reference in the bottom portion of Table 6-1. Of these only Chile presents conceptual problems, because its demographic transition seems to have spanned a very long period separated by a time of stable birth rates; nevertheless, major natality decline has clearly occurred there and is ongoing. (There are four other nations that do not fit our requirements completely but have had some decline. These are discussed

---

[a]In Chapter 2, Germany was considered to be in "central Europe." In these hypotheses, however, central Europe is not explicitly dealt with. Germany was thought to be closer to "northwestern" Europe than "eastern" Europe, both in terms of geography and sociodemographic trends during the natality decline.

Table 6-1

R^2 Values Resulting from Fitting Various Functional Forms to Declines in the Crude Birth Rate (CBR) of European and Latin American Countries

Country or Region	Functional Form			
	$1ny=a+bx$	$y=a+bx$	$y=a+bx^{1.5}$	$y=a+bx^2$
Belgium	.936	.957	.972	.955
Denmark	.913	.944	.979	.979
England and Wales	.945	.981	.989	.971
France	.941	.949	.912	.864
Germany	.856	.904	.963	.982
Ireland	.833	.830	.831	.826
Netherlands	.936	.961	.974	.959
Norway	.826	.882	.945	.970
Scotland	.956	.979	.984	.965
Sweden	.869	.921	.964	.975
Switzerland	.888	.901	.925	.918
Northwestern Europe, mean	.900	.928	.949	.942
Northwestern Europe, median	.913	.944	.964	.965
Number of "best fits"	1	1	5½	3½
Italy	.948	.970	.965	.935
Portugal	.828	.827	.753	.689
Spain	.922	.946	.964	.950
Southern Europe, mean	.899	.914	.894	.858
Southern Europe, median	.828	.946	.964	.935
Number of "best fits"	1	1	1	0
Argentina	.959	.966	.953	.908
Chile (long series)[a]	.869	.897	.919	.911
Costa Rica	.887	.906	.965	.977
Cuba (long series)[a]	.851	.815	.670	.605
El Salvador[b]	.881[b]	.891[b]	.909[b]	.891[b]
Guatemala[b]	.866[b]	.883[b]	.917[b]	.919[b]
Guyana[b]	.734[b]	.747[b]	.841[b]	.897[b]
Jamaica	.813	.819	.810	.766
Panama[b]	.930[b]	.933[b]	.933[b]	.902[b]
Puerto Rico	.954	.961	.920	.857
Trinidad and Tobago	.880	.895	.923	.918
Uruguay	.890	.873	.764	.665
Latin America, mean	.887	.891	.870	.833
Latin America, median	.881	.895	.919	.891
Number of "best fits"	2	3	3	1

Table 6-1 (notes)

[a]See Table 6-3 for periods.

[b]Doubtful cases excluded from summary statistics below.

Note: For information on time periods used, boundaries, and data sources, see the notes to Tables 6-2 and 6-3. R^2 is the coefficient of determination used here only as a measure of goodness of fit; "*ln*" is "natural logarithm of"; y is the crude birth rate; a and b are constants fitted by the regression procedure; x is the time in years since the onset of natality decline as determined by the rules defined in the text. The first functional form is based on constant percentage decline; the second is based on constant absolute decline; the third and fourth assume rising degrees of accelerating absolute decline. A "best fit" is a country for which the R^2 of a given functional form is higher than any other functional form shown for that country.

in more detail later in this chapter, in the context of hypothesis 3. El Salvador and Guatemala have lowered the CBR by over 15 percent, but are still above 40. Guyana has a 15%+ CBR decline and is below 40, but still above 35. Panama has a CBR near 35 but no 15% drop. These four are marked by a footnote reference in subsequent tables.)

Determining the period of natality decline. For the sample of countries with natality declines, it is necessary to define for each the time at which the natality decline of the demographic transition began. All data pertaining to years before 1874 were excluded from analysis—the year 1874 was included to allow for a three-year average centered on 1875. This practice eliminates the difficulties that stem from the differences in the dates at which reliable natality data series begin in European countries and in a few Latin American countries with early natality declines. Latin America is hardly affected by the removal of pre-1875 data, since little information is available. In Europe before that time, natality declines, where they can be observed, were generally slower and much more irregular than those of subsequent periods. The European rates of decline are therefore higher than would be the case if earlier data were included; this works against the relevant hypotheses, especially 1a. Alternative calculations made for France, the nation with one of the longest and most consistent pre-1875 natality declines, showed that the reduction of the crude birth rate is about 20 percent faster if counted from 1875 rather than 1820, the date at which a clear pattern of decline emerges. (Previous to 1820, possible disturbances of the Napoleonic wars make the data difficult to interpret.) Similarly, early natality declines in the Scandinavian countries were quite slow.

As a general principle, the midyear of the maximum three-year moving average was taken as the onset of natality decline, provided that the particular country had good annual data. For Argentina, Cuba, Chile, and Uruguay the midyear of the maximum five-year estimate (Collver, 1965) was used instead. All other countries showing natality reduction have the requisite annual data, assuming no significant trends in Latin American countries (excepting the four noted above) before World War II. In each case this maximum was promptly followed by sustained natality declines for a number of years.

Defining the end of the natality decline was difficult, since it was not always clear whether the experience of European countries should be extended beyond World War II or terminated during the Depression. After some experimentation, the end of the natality decline was defined as the midyear of the first three-year moving average that remained an unsurpassed minimum for 15 years or more, provided it was 20.5 or lower (could be rounded to 20). If this procedure yielded no conclusive terminal date, the last annual datum was defined as the end of the series, on the assumption that natality decline was still in progress. For the sake of uniformity, five-year averages are used for the entire series of birth rates of Argentina, Chile, Cuba, and Uruguay.

These rules tend to maximize rates of decline in northwestern Europe, by excluding from consideration the years of World War II and the postwar natality recovery; this is a conservative procedure relative to hypothesis 1a. On the other hand, the same rules required that the natality declines in Italy, Portugal, and Spain be carried through World War II. To see if this produced a misleadingly slow rate, I undertook an alternative set of calculations utilizing the Depression natality lows as the terminal years for Italy and Spain; in both cases the longer period actually had a slightly faster rate of decline. Portugal had no pronounced natality dip during the Depression but did reach a plateau in the early 1940s, while the rules defined above carried the natality decline up to the present. If the 1940s minimum were taken as the end of the natality decline, the apparent reduction rate would be much higher than that obtained with the present methods; however, this would involve the assumption that the demographic transition can end with a crude birth rate of 23.7 (observed in 1941). Where Europe is concerned, the rules are not biased in favor of hypotheses 1a-1c; probably the opposite is closer to the truth.

In Latin America the rules indicated that natality declines extend up to the present. Only one nation (Uruguay) had an estimated CBR of 25 or lower before World War II (Collver, 1965; Rothman, 1970). Alternative calculations made for Uruguay revealed that the rate of decline is .457 per year for the period 1897-1947 and .318 per year using data to the present (as the rules required). There are no serious problems in defining the end of natality declines in Latin America, since none are terminated early and since any bias would appear to minimize Latin American decline rates and act against the hypotheses.

Obtaining a measure of natality decline. It was decided to fit lines to the observed CBR series and to use a parameter from that line as a measure of slope. This method was preferred since it utilizes all of the available data points, and allows the calculation of rates of decline for Latin American countries that have not completed the demographic transition. The problem is then to get a functional form that is a close fit to reality, and one that is likely to be a valid projection for those societies with only a partial natality decline thus far. Initially the CBR series for every relevant European and Latin American country were graphed. It was readily apparent that some previously suspected regularities did not occur; for instance there was very little indication of an inverted S-curve—natality decline did seem to begin slowly, but it then tended to accelerate right up to the end of the demographic transition. Preliminary work suggested four likely curves. One of these assumes constant percentage change; another constant absolute change; and two others assume various degrees of accelerating absolute change. Each of these four forms was fitted to every relevant period of national natality decline. The results appear in Table 6-1.

Among these choices, the best fit is obtained with the functional form $y = a + bx^{1.5}$. Presumably, one could do even better by using an iterative procedure to fix the value of the exponent of x. Nevertheless, it was decided to use the value of the linear regression coefficient (b in $y = a + bx$) as the primary measure of rate of natality decline.

Although this model did not yield the best fit, there are three persuasive arguments in favor of its adoption. First, the linear regression coefficient is easy to interpret as a statistical estimate of the average annual decline in CBR. Second, despite giving poorer fits on the average than the accelerating models, the linear assumption yielded fewer really poor fits, and none below an R^2 of .75. Finally, since the Latin American countries have not completed natality decline, a chief concern was not to *over*estimate the likely future reductions in the CBR and thus bias the measure of decline in favor of the hypotheses. The assumption of constant absolute decrements in the CBR is a more conservative estimate of subsequent natality reductions than the "better-fitting" assumptions of accelerating absolute decline.

A secondary means of testing hypotheses 1a-1c uses the regression coefficient (b) based on the constant percentage change model (b in $y = a + bx$). As shown above, the pace of decline described by this curve has not been typical; rather, it is a still more conservative assumption about the likely rate of future natality decline in the Latin American countries of interest. This measure is used because some might argue that recent absolute declines in the CBR in several Latin American countries, often beginning from very high levels, are too rapid to be continued for very long.

Results of the Analysis of
Declines in the CBR

Test of hypotheses 1a-1c as stated. Table 6-2 is presented to demonstrate the relative homogeneity of rates of natality decline in northwestern Europe, and thus to justify treating these as a group, as hypothesis 1a requires. Note that in terms of absolute decline only three of the eleven units are outside the range .26 – .37 points per year, these being France and Ireland (slow) and Germany

Table 6-2

Comparative Rates of Decline in CBR within Northwestern Europe

Country	Period	Absolute Annual Decline	Percent Annual Decline
Belgium	1875-1936	.281	1.18
Denmark	1885-1934	.307	1.24
England and Wales	1876-1934	.365	1.50
France	1876-1938	.153	.75
Germany	1875-1932	.415	1.51
Ireland	1875-1939	.085	.38
Netherlands	1876-1936	.264	.93
Norway	1878-1935	.291	1.23
Scotland	1875-1939	.290	1.14
Sweden	1875-1934	.282	1.26
Switzerland	1876-1938	.271	1.20

Note: Territories are of date except Ireland, which is the island of Ireland throughout. Boundary changes in the above nations during the period of interest were generally minor. The most severe adjustments were in Germany after World War I; an examination of partial alternative series provided by Kuczynski (1928) for pre- and post-World-War-I territories suggests that little bias is introduced by using Germany of date. For data sources and other information, see the note to Table 6-3.

(fast). In percentage terms, seven of the eleven nations have annual declines estimated between .93 percent and 1.26 percent, the others being France and Ireland (slow) and England and Wales and Germany (fast).

Preliminary investigation revealed that the patterns of natality decline in Latin America tended to be very different before and after World War II. Therefore one set of figures ("long series") refers to median and mean rates of natality decline for the respective periods appropriate to each country; these include four instances of prewar natality decline. An alternative set of calculations ("postwar") excludes Argentina and Uruguay, where the major portion of birth rate reduction had already been completed before World War II, and uses only data for the postwar phases of natality decline in Chile and Cuba, where the trend is apparent both before and after World War II. The countries with postwar birth rate declines only generate one set of calculations and are identically represented in the Latin American summary statistics, whether for the "long" or "postwar" series.

Resultant comparisons of the rates of decline in the crude birth rate in northwestern Europe, Italy, Iberia, and Latin America appear in Table 6-3. It is immediately apparent that postwar natality declines in Latin America have been much more rapid than those of earlier periods. It is also clear that Latin American countries have reduced natality more dramatically in absolute than in

Table 6-3
Comparative Rates of Decline in the CBR in Europe and Latin America

Area	Period	Absolute Annual Decline	Percent Annual Decline
Northwestern Europe			
Belgium	1875-1936	.281	1.18
Denmark	1885-1934	.307	1.24
England and Wales	1876-1934	.365	1.50
France	1876-1938	.153	.75
Germany	1875-1932	.415	1.51
Ireland	1875-1939	.085	.38
Netherlands	1876-1936	.264	.93
Norway	1878-1935	.291	1.23
Scotland	1875-1939	.290	1.14
Sweden	1875-1934	.282	1.26
Switzerland	1876-1938	.271	1.20
Northwestern Europe			
Median	c.1875-c.1935	.291	1.20
Unweighted mean	c.1875-c.1935	.273	1.12
Mean weighted by 1900 pop.	c.1875-c.1935	.313	1.24
Southern Europe			
Italy	1884-1953	.286	1.02
Portugal	1923-1970	.229	.88
Spain	1885-1954	.243	.86
Latin America			
Argentina[a]	1877-1969	.305	.93
Chile[a]	1882-1970	.161	.40
Chile, postwar[b]	1956-1970	.683	2.10
Costa Rica	1955-1972	1.133	2.78
Cuba[a]	1907-1969	.298	.84
Cuba, postwar[b]	1952-1967	.327	1.12
El Salvador[c]	1957-1972	.686	1.49
Guatemala[c]	1949-1971	.500	1.02
Guayana[c]	1953-1968	.448	1.10
Jamaica	1959-1972	.606	1.61
Panama[c]	1961-1972	.438	1.13
Puerto Rico	1949-1972	.900	2.70
Trinidad and Tobago	1954-1972	.938	3.18
Uruguay	1859-1969	.318	1.08
Latin America, long series			
Median	Various	.474	1.12

Table 6-3 (cont.)

Area	Period	Absolute Annual Decline	Percent Annual Decline
Unweighted mean	periods as	.561	1.52
Mean weighted by 1970 pop.	stated above	.396	1.08
Latin America, postwar			
Median	Various	.552	1.31
Unweighted mean	periods as	.666	1.82
Mean weighted by 1970 pop.	stated above	.482	1.68

[a]These data were not included in the summary statistics labeled "postwar."

[b]These data were not included in the summary statistics labeled "long-series."

[c]The four doubtful cases (see text) are included in the summary statistics, since their exclusion would favor the hypothesis.

Note: Data for European countries are from Kuczynski (1928, 1931) supplemented by United Nations *Demographic Yearbooks* beginning about 1930. Data for Argentina and Cuba are from Collver (1965) up to 1950, from the United Nations (1969) for 1950-65, and from the United Nations *Demographic Yearbook*, 1970, thereafter. Pre-1950 data for Uruguay are from Rothman (1969), 1950-65 data are from the United Nations (1969), and later data are from the United Nations *Demographic Yearbook*, 1970. Pre-1950 data for Chile are from Collver (1965). All other Latin American data are from United Nations *Demographic Yearbooks* and the United Nations (1974). Puerto Rican rates are corrected for underregistration according to estimates made by Vasquez (1968). All territories are of date except Ireland, which is the island of Ireland throughout. Years excluded due to war time disruption and subsequent natality recovery periods were as follows: 1915-21 for Belgium, England-Wales, France, Germany, Ireland (because of Northern Ireland), and Scotland; 1916-21 and 1941-47 for Italy; 1938-39 and 1941-42 for Spain. All data are annual observations except those for Argentina, Cuba, Chile (long series), and Uruguay, which are five-year observations.

percentage terms. Thus we find hypotheses 1a-1c strongly supported on the basis of absolute rates and postwar Latin American trends. The hypotheses are also confirmed, but not quite so strikingly, with absolute rates and the "long series" or with percentage rates and the "postwar" Latin American data. The least favorable outcomes are obtained from examination of the percentage rates with "long series" calculations: Hypothesis 1c (Iberian-Latin American comparisons) is still clearly supported; however, both 1a and 1b (comparisons between Latin America and northwestern Europe or Italy) meet with inconclusive results. Subject to this exception the data tend to confirm the hypotheses strongly.

The interpretation of these findings rests on two questions: (1) whether absolute or percentage rates of natality decline are more realistic, especially in terms of which Latin American countries are more likely to maintain in the future; (2) whether the prewar or postwar period exhibits the rates of natality decline more representative of the total Latin American experience. In regard to the first question, we have already examined evidence (Table 6-1) that past natality declines have actually tended to accelerate even in absolute terms over time. The (nonaccelerating) absolute rate was chosen because it was conservative relative to known experience. The even more conservative percentage rates were added for comparative purposes, and as extra protection in view of the exceedingly fast rates of natality reduction noted in many Latin American countries thus far. One could construct a good argument in favor of the meaningfulness of absolute rates of decline, but the more interesting theoretical issue involves the second question—the contrast between pre- and postwar conditions.

A possible modification of the hypotheses. From the analysis, it became apparent that there were really two distinct periods of natality decline in Latin America. Before World War II the virtually complete natality reductions in Argentina and Uruguay proceeded slowly, as did the partial natality decline in Chile and Cuba. After World War II, natality declines are generally much more rapid, including the "second-stage" drops in Chile and Cuba. Hypotheses 1a-1c are strongly confirmed for the post-World-War-II era, but not for the earlier period.

This divergence makes sense if the causal foundation behind hypotheses 1a-1c is recalled. Originally it was asserted that natality declines in Latin America should be faster than in the northwestern and southern European nations, because mortality reduction and/or socioeconomic development had been more rapid and because mortality reduction-socioeconomic development is thought to be the primary cause of reduction of the birth rate. Rates of mortality reduction and other dimensions of development have been accelerating over time in Latin America (see pp. 95-104). Thus, the assumed causes of rapid demographic transition are largely confined to a more recent period. Were hypotheses 1a-1c to be rewritten, this fact could be taken into account and the assertions could be restricted to avoid the pre-World-War-II natality declines—i.e., Argentina and Uruguay would be virtually eliminated from consideration, as would the early parts of the birth rate declines in Chile and Cuba. These modified hypotheses would still test the assumed causal structure, and are much more convincingly supported.

More Refined Measures of Natality

Overview. The crude birth rate (CBR) is a rough indication of natality that can be severely distorted by extraneous factors, notably the age-sex structure. In the long run, the CBR should provide a good indication of major trends. In order to demonstrate that findings would be at least as favorable to hypotheses 1a-1c with better natality measures, a separate analysis was undertaken using refined natality indicators. Unfortunately, such information is not available for many countries. It is even more disturbing that the calculation of the presumed "superior" measures necessitates new assumptions or the use of new data (e.g., to control for age-sex structure, one needs to know the population by age and sex and something about the pattern of age-specific fertility). Sometimes these additional pieces of information may themselves contain so much error that in the end the CBR may have been a better indicator. With these cautions in mind, we will proceed to see what can be done with the data at hand.

Gross reproduction rates (GRR): availability. The main effort was directed at obtaining times-series of GRRs for as many of the countries in Tables 6-2 and 6-3 as possible. The GRR is a directly standardized measure of natality which, although more difficult to obtain, is much preferable to indirectly standardized rates when the populations that must be compared have different patterns of age-specific fertility. This is the case with comparisons that extend from Europe to Latin America.

GRR data are available for five of our eleven northwestern European nations over most or all of the periods of natality decline. In southern Europe, the data are unfortunately limited to the latter phases of the natality declines, but this partial information can be found for all three countries. The quality and availability of GRRs in Latin America are very uneven from country to country, but very little information exists prior to 1950. There are reasonably good series for five of the twelve Latin American nations of Table 6-3.

GRR: Graphic presentation. As a first attempt to analyze the trends, graphs were made of available GRRs which fell into the periods covered by the CBR declines as listed in Table 6-3. For Latin America any data after 1950 were also included, regardless of when the CBR began to decline; the reason for this modification lies in the fact that in some cases the GRR decline seems to have begun several years before or after the corresponding event as judged by the CBR. Results appear in Figure 6-1, which illustrates several points. First, it does appear that natality decline in Spain and Portugal proceeded more slowly than in the five northwestern European nations included in the graph. This assures that if hypothesis 1a holds, 1c will hold as well. Unfortunately, GRRs for Italy are not available until 1931, a time when the natality level was already quite low; this leaves hypothesis 1b largely indeterminate. However, Livi-Bacci (1966) has calculated an indirectly standardized natality measure that strongly suggests slow decline in Italy before 1931. Turning to the crucial Latin American countries, we see that GRRs in four of the five were virtually trendless or tended to rise slightly during the 1950s. This may be partially or wholly due to improving registration of births. In Puerto Rico, which has long had relatively good statistics and where the data have been closely examined and refined by Vasquez (1968), there is a steady decline from 1950. After 1960 there is exceedingly rapid natality decline in all five Latin American countries, with the possible exception of Panama, where the GRR drop is more moderate.

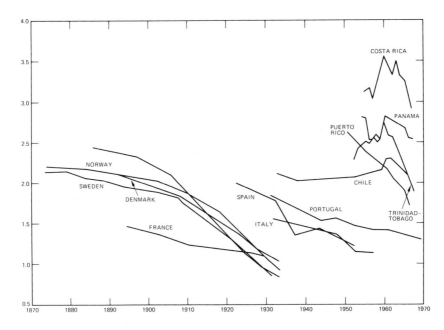

Figure 6-1. Gross Reproduction Rates During Natality Declines in Northwestern and Southern Europe and Latin America. Source: See Table 6-4.

Rates of decline of the GRRs. A comparison of rates of decline of the GRRs was also performed. Since these "series" consist of irregular and often infrequent observations, the line-fitting procedure used with the CBRs is inappropriate. Instead, initial and terminal dates of GRR decline were defined under the same rules previously applied to the CBR data, except that years back to 1870 were included and any available aggregations of years or single years were used in lieu of three-year moving averages. The rate of natality decline was then defined as the difference between initial and terminal GRRs divided by the number of elapsed years.

Unfortunately, the incomplete data for southern Europe and Latin America prior to World War II makes comparisons with the results for the CBR difficult. To facilitate comparison with the original CBR findings, Table 6-4 presents the results of the GRR analysis, together with the data on the CBR for the same countries but for the periods of CBR decline (which are somewhat different). The original rates of CBR decline for Chile have been replaced with statistics calculated on the basis of the post-World-War-II period only, thus conforming more closely to the observable period of GRR decline. The results appear in Table 6-4.

Hypotheses 1a and 1b are strongly confirmed using either the GRR or the

Table 6-4
Comparison of Rates of Natality Decline Based on CBR and GRR

Area	Observed GRR Decline Period	Absolute Annual Decline		Percent Annual Decline	
		GRR	CBR	GRR	CBR
Denmark	1878-84-1933	.023	.31	1.50	1.24
England and Wales	1870-72-1933	.023	.36	1.57	1.50
France	1892-96-1935	.011	.15	.91	.75
Germany	1881-90-1931	.035	.42	2.28	1.51
Norway	1871-76-1935	.022	.29	1.51	1.23
Sweden	1876-80-1935	.024	.28	1.71	1.26
Northwestern Europe					
Median	See above	.023	.30	1.54	1.25
Mean (unweighted)	See above	.023	.30	1.58	1.25
Mean (weighted by population c.1920)	See above	.025	.32	1.69	1.29
Italy	1931-1958	.017	.29	1.28	1.02
Portugal	1930-31-1969	.014	.23	.92	.88
Spain	1922-1950-54	.027	.24	1.70	.86
Chile	1961-1967	.158	.55	4.92	1.94
Costa Rica	1961-1967	.070	.98	3.30	2.45
Panama[a]	1960-1970	.035	.37	1.30	.93
Puerto Rico	1950-1966	.053	.80	2.43	2.44
Trinidad and Tobago	1954-1969	.069	1.16	3.22	3.49
Latin America					
Median	See above	.069	.80	3.22	2.44
Mean (unweighted)	See above	.077	.77	3.03	2.25
Mean (weighted by population 1970)	See above	.116	.65	3.87	2.09

[a]Possible natality decline.

Note: See the notes to Tables 6-2 and 6-3 for boundary information, periods of observation, and sources of CBR data. GRR data for northwestern Europe before 1932 are from Kuczynski (1936), and later data are from United Nations *Demographic Yearbooks*. Initial data for Italy and Spain are from Kuczynski (1936). Other pre-1942 data for Spain are from the United Nations *Demographic Yearbook*, 1949-50. The 1969 GRR for Portugal was calculated from age-specific births and population of females by age given in the United Nations *Demographic Yearbook*, 1970. All other data for southern Europe are from *Population Index*. Data for Chile, Trinidad and Tobago, and Panama are from United Nations *Demographic Yearbooks* supplemented by *Population Index*. Data for Costa Rica are from Huyck (1970), and for Puerto Rico from Vasquez (1968), supplemented by *Population Index*. Where an aggregation was used as an initial or terminal datum, this is indicated by a dash and separating the first year of the aggregation from the last two digits of the last year; e.g., 1870-74-1900 means "the initial observation is for 1870-74 and the last observation is the year 1900."

CBR figures. The only minor anomalies are found in the rather fast natality decline in Germany and the rather slow one in Panama; this too occurs with both natality measures. Otherwise, the comparison between the Latin American nations and northwestern Europe or Italy is striking, and supportive of the hypotheses. Turning to the Iberian countries (Hypothesis 1c), however, there is a problem, in that Spain appears to have a much faster natality reduction when the GRR data are substituted for the CBRs. Natality declines in Latin America are still faster, especially in absolute terms, but hypothesis 1c would have to be modified to exclude the word "much" if the GRR findings were taken as definitive. These results may be misleading, however, because the GRR series for Spain omits the period before 1922, during which natality seems to have been falling slowly (the CBR fell from 36.3 in 1885 to 30.4 in 1922—see also Livi-Bacci, 1968a, 1968b). In general, the GRR data suggest that the conclusions previously made on the basis of CBRs would not have to be greatly altered if age-sex standardized measures were available for comparable periods.

Limits to interpretation of the GRR data. Although there is no reason to believe that use of more refined natality measures would upset the findings, it should be noted that the selective availability of GRR information works in favor of the hypotheses by essentially excluding pre-World-War-II Latin America. Thus, the GRR data, if viewed alone, does not really test hypotheses 1a-1c as written, but what we have called the "modified" versions of these (see pp. 88-89). To be completely fair, one would have to substitute "post-World-War-II Latin America" for "Latin America" in hypotheses 1a-1c. As discussed above, this change makes the hypotheses much easier to defend and, for causal purposes, is virtually the same as the original versions.

Hypotheses 2a and 2b

Overview

Hypotheses 2a and 2b state that natality decline rates are directly related to rates of change in mortality and socioeconomic indicators, respectively. Country units are used for comparison. However, because the previous analysis has suggested a meaningful division between pre- and post-World-War-II periods, some consideration is also given to differences over time intervals, in addition to cross-national variation.

Mortality Decline Rate as a
Predictor of Natality Decline Rate

Crude Death Rates. Fortunately, and thanks largely to Collver (1965), estimates of the CDR are available for many countries, despite the frequent lack of usable official statistics. By supplementing these data with information from the United Nations and Rothman's (1969) estimates for Uruguay, a fairly long series can be obtained for all twelve relevant Latin American countries (those identified as having confirmed or possible natality decline).

Measuring the rate of CDR decline still presents some difficult problems. In almost every instance, CDR reduction is already under way at or near the beginning of the data series. This makes a line-fitting procedure similar to that used for the CBRs awkward, since limited segments of the CDR decline are observed and the rates appear to be dependent on the segment available. For instance, Uruguay, which never has an estimated CDR above 15, could not possibly lower its death rate very much during the time covered by the data. With this in mind, an alternate method, described in Chapter 5 as "benchmarks," was utilized. In this case an effort was made to estimate the time required to move from CDR = 30 to CDR = 10 and, alternatively, the time required to move from CDR = 30 to CDR = 15.

Even the construction of the two "benchmark" measures involves very serious drawbacks, however, which were never fully resolved. The difficulty arises from the fact that there is no wide range of crude death rates through which most nations have passed during the periods for which data are available. Eight of the twelve Latin American countries of interest have never recorded a CDR as high as 30, and several have never even been close. Thus it was necessary to make some assumption about rates of decline in mortality for periods prior to the beginnings of the data series.

When the CDR series (including the projected segments) had been constructed and benchmark mortality decline rates derived, it was found that there was only a very weak relationship with rates of natality (CBR) decline. These overwhelmingly negative findings persist whether or not the somewhat unusual cases of Argentina and Uruguay are included. Furthermore, it makes little difference whether one considers the natality declines in Chile and Cuba to be long-term or confined to the post-World-War-II period. In the interests of economy these results are reported but not presented in detail.

Expectation of life at birth. To ascertain whether the negative findings obtained above might have been due to incompleteness or poor quality of the crude death rate data, a reanalysis was undertaken using the expectation of life at birth (for both sexes). Fortunately, these data series are quite complete in that a fairly broad range of mortality decline can be observed in most countries. Only Cuba and Uruguay are excluded for lack of data. The measure of rapidity of mortality decline chosen was the estimated number of years needed to increase expectation of life at birth (e_0) from 35 to 50. These benchmarks were picked because they represented the widest range of mortality decline that could be observed for most of the relevant countries.

Again there were some problems in that five countries never had an estimated

e_0 as low as 35, but since all of these were quite close at some time, there was relatively little danger in making some blanket assumption about early improvements in expectation of life. In this case, I assumed that any increase in e_0 prior to the beginning of the data series was between 1.5 and 3.0 years per decade. The period to which this assumption is applied is *circa* 1900, and observed mortality declines were generally within this range.

The results of this process, together with the rank order of rapidity of mortality decline (e_0 increase) and comparative rates of natality decline, appear in Table 6-5. The rankings in mortality decline rate were established on the assumption that where a range of years is estimated to move from $e_0 = 35$ to $e_0 = 50$, the actual number of years is close to the midpoint of the range. Jamaica and Puerto Rico are both ranked as 8-1/2 since the midpoint of the range of years for each is between 47 and 48.

Again, various techniques were tried to assess the association between rates of mortality and natality decline, with uniformly negative results. Including or excluding Argentina, the only country in the table experiencing most of its natality decline before World War II, makes little difference. Nor does the use of the postwar natality decline in Chile versus the longer time period change the findings appreciably. Also, it makes no difference whether the rates of mortality and natality decline are considered rank-order or interval level for purposes of correlation. The correlations are always small and often negative (the reverse of that expected).

Acceleration of mortality decline. There is one respect in which mortality and natality decline rates are closely related: both tend to accelerate over time regardless of the country observed, subject only to the obvious ceiling-floor effects. For natality, the "acceleration" is more apparent if pre- and post-World-War-II periods are contrasted (see pp. 87-89), but an acceleration in *percentage* natality decline is implied by the good results of the linear fit to CBR series (see Table 6-1). The acceleration in mortality decline is apparent using either CDR or e_0 data. Table 6-6 illustrates the acceleration by displaying decadel change in each of these measures in relevant Latin American countries. In part I of the table, absolute declines in the CDR of over 4 points have been underlined to emphasize the trend of acceleration. There are no such declines until 1900, none of over 6 points until 1920, and none of over 8 points until 1940. The largest decadel decline, 8.9 points, was not observed until the most recent period (in El Salvador).

The pattern of increasingly rapid improvements in mortality measures is even more apparent from the data on expectation of life at birth in part II of Table 6-6. Although the increasing availability of data in more recent times is problematic, the pattern of acceleration is too obvious to be obscured.

Natality declines in Latin America are more recent and less widespread than mortality declines, but wherever both trends are established, they have tended to

Table 6-5
Comparisons of Rates of Increase in Expectation of Life at Birth and Rates of Natality Decline

Country	Approximate Year at Which $e_0 = 35$	Approximate Year at Which $e_0 = 50$	Years Needed to Increase e_0 from 35 to 50 Years	Rank on Rapidity of e_0 Increase	Rate of Natality Decline CBR Absolute	CBR Percent	GRR Absolute	GRR Percent
Guatemala	1944	1966	22	1	.500	1.02	N.A.	N.A.
Guyana	1922	1945	23	2	.448	1.10	N.A.	N.A.
Panama[a]	1924-1927	1950	23-26	3	.438	1.13	.035	1.30
El Salvador	1927	1953	26	4	.686	1.49	N.A.	N.A.
Costa Rica	1916	1942	36	5	1.133	2.78	.070	3.30
Argentina	1879-1887	1922	35-43	6	.305	.93	N.A.	N.A.
Chile	1914	1952	38	7	.161[b]	.40[b]	.158	4.92
Jamaica	1883-1897	1937	40-54	8½	.606	1.61	N.A.	N.A.
Puerto Rico	1888-1899	1943	44-55	8½	.900	2.70	.053	2.43
Trinidad and Tobago	1884-1893	1942	49-58	10	.938	3.18	.069	3.49

[a]Possible natality decline.

[b]Based on the post-World-War II period the rates of CBR decline for Chile would be .683 (absolute) and 2.10 (percent); the Chilean GRR series is already limited to the postwar period.

Note: Data on expectation of life at birth for Chile, Costa Rica, El Salvador, Guatemala, and Panama are taken from Arriaga (1968) as available. Supplementary e_0 data for these countries and all data for the others are from United Nations *Demographic Yearbooks*. Interpolation was used to estimate the time needed to increase e_0 from 35 to 50 years; see the above text for additional information. Data on natality declines are from Tables 6-3 and 6-4, respectively.

proceed with increasing rapidity over time, especially since the postwar period began. If this longitudinal association of mortality and natality decline rates is a product of the causal relationships posited by transition theory (and the present model), countries beginning natality declines in the future should also move very quickly to lower levels. This would, of course, provide relief from present high rates of population growth, which in turn were produced by the accelerating mortality decline.

Summary: hypothesis 2a. As stated, hypothesis 2a has been convincingly refuted. While this may be partly due to difficulties in measuring rates of change, the data are too clear to be dismissed lightly. However, both natality and mortality declines tend to be more rapid in more recent times. If time periods were taken as the relevant units of analysis for hypothesis 2a (rather than countries), there would certainly be a tendency for rates of decline in these vital rates to be associated. Although I have not tried to assess the causes of the acceleration of change, there are undoubtedly factors correlated with time itself that have been affecting most or all of the countries in question and facilitating faster mortality *and* natality reductions in more recent periods. The regression analysis reported in Chapter 7, treats each temporal observation for a given country as a separate unit and concentrates on the post-World-War-II period.

Socioeconomic Development Indicators
as Predictors of Natality Decline Rate

Nature of the data. Hypothesis 2b predicts an association between rate of socioeconomic development and rate of natality decline. There are a very large number of indicators that could be interpreted as measures of development. Unfortunately, it is impossible to obtain reasonably long historical series for the great majority of them. Three have therefore been chosen, tapping what appear to be conceptually distinct aspects of the development process: school enrollment, urbanization, and national product.

Rates of change of socioeconomic indicators. The evaluation of hypothesis 2b encountered methodological obstacles that rendered a fair test extremely difficult. These problems resulted from an inability to control two complicating factors in calculating rates of change of development indicators: lag times and levels of variables.

A test of transition theory requires some lag between socioeconomic trends and the natality changes that should result. Unfortunately, the findings are highly dependent upon the particular lag chosen. Natality declines in Latin America have occurred mainly after 1955. Significant socioeconomic development began earlier, however. Thus if the lag time chosen were ten years and the

Table 6-6
Decadal Improvements in Mortality Measures

Part I: Absolute Declines in the CDR

Country	1862	1872	1882	1892	1902	1912	1922	1932	1942	1952
					Decade Beginning with the Five-Year Period Centered on:					
Argentina	1.0	1.6	4.0	3.5	4.9	3.7	2.4	1.2	1.5	.4
Chile	.3	.1	1.2	1.1	.1	.2	6.8	4.4	6.4	1.9
Costa Rica				.1	1.6	2.0	3.7	4.1	6.7	2.2
Cuba					2.3	2.1	6.0	2.4		
El Salvador[a]					-1.4	-1.7	.1	4.2	8.5	8.9
Guatemala[a]					1.6	-.7	2.0	4.2	5.1	6.7
Guyana[a]						0	5.3	3.4	6.4	4.9
Jamaica						-1.2	6.3	3.5	2.9	3.0
Panama[a]					2.0	1.7	2.2	2.4	3.6	
Puerto Rico							-.1	4.8	7.3	2.1
Trinidad and Tobago						3.9	3.4	2.7	4.9	4.0
Uruguay					.8	-.1	212	.8	2.0	.3

Part II: Absolute Increases in e_0

Country	Decade Beginning with the Year:										
	1860	1870	1880	1890	1900	1910	1920	1930	1940	1950	1960
Chile	1.7				1.5	.3	4.7	2.9	<u>10.4</u>	<u>8.0</u>	<u>6.6</u>
Costa Rica		1.0	1.5	1.5	1.0	4.2	5.1	<u>6.8</u>	<u>6.8</u>	<u>6.3</u>	
El Salvador[a]								<u>8.8</u>	<u>9.7</u>	<u>8.8</u>	
Guatemala[a]				.5	.6	.9	1.1	3.8	<u>10.3</u>	<u>8.8</u>	
Guyana[a]						3.4	<u>6.7</u>	<u>6.1</u>	<u>6.8</u>	<u>7.1</u>	
Jamaica								<u>8.1</u>	<u>6.2</u>	<u>6.1</u>	
Panama[a]								<u>6.5</u>	<u>7.8</u>	<u>11.3</u>	
Puerto Rico					2.3	b	b	b	<u>14.5</u>	<u>9.0</u>	2.7
Trinidad and Tobago						- .9	<u>6.1</u>	5.7	5.6	<u>7.9</u>	

[a]Possible natality decline.

[b]Data indicate a total increase of 7.6 years in e_0 between 1910 and 1940.

Note: CDR is the crude death rate or number of deaths per 1000 population. CDR data for Guyana, Jamaica, Puerto Rico, and Trinidad and Tobago are from United Nations *Demographic Yearbooks*; for these, the column labeled "1912" is the decade beginning with 1911-13, rather than 1910-14. Other CDR data are from Collver (1965) as available. "e_0" is the expectation of life at birth in years. e_0 data for Guyana, Jamaica, Puerto Rico, and Trinidad and Tobago are from Arriaga (1968). Interpolation has been used with the raw e_0 data. For emphasis, CDR declines of 4.0 points or more and e_0 increases of 6.0 years or more in a decade are underlined. A minus sign indicates an increase in the CDR.

1935-46 changes in development measures were compared with natality declines during 1945-55, one would obtain much different results than with a longer lag (and for the ten-year lag the findings would have to be very negative).

On the other hand, the use of any fixed time period to measure change implies that initial levels of development indicators would be different for various countries. This would greatly affect the crucial rates of change needed to test the hypothesis. Thus, once a country achieves a high degree of urbanization or school enrollment, it is incapable of showing rapid rates of change in these variables. Almost the opposite situation holds for measures of national product: at higher initial levels subsequent changes are usually greater, regardless of whether percentages or absolute rates of change are used.

Probably the best solution to these problems would be to assume that one can speak of the rate at which a certain aspect of development proceeds in a given country, and to measure this quantity by the benchmark technique. Then, provided that the observed period of natality decline was subsequent to the observed changes in development, one could compare the rate of one aspect of development in a given country with the rate of natality decline. The levels of the development measure would be controlled and the lag times would be left to the data to determine—the lag would simply be the time between the first benchmark and the onset of natality decline. (In testing this hypothesis, an effort is made to avoid any specific lag assumption. In Chapter 7 various lag times are tried on an experimental basis.)

Unfortunately, only the school enrollment data offer sufficient coverage to allow the effective use of the benchmark technique. For the others the principal measure of rate of development is the change (either percentage or absolute or both) in an indicator over the longest period for which comparative data can be obtained. It is hoped that this approximates the findings that would be obtained with benchmarks. Because it is not possible to get sufficient data on school enrollment before 1920, urbanization before 1930, or national product before 1950, and since natality decline rates should be measured subsequent to their presumed causes, only post-World-War-II natality declines are used. This effectively eliminates Argentina and Uruguay from analysis, since natality was falling before 1900 and was fairly low by 1950. For Chile and Cuba, the rate of natality decline is then based on the second phase reductions which began in the 1950s.

Results: hypothesis 2b. Table 6-7 shows rates of socioeconomic development compared with rates of natality decline. There is some support for hypothesis 2b. Increases in school enrollment are related to natality decline, but only if the benchmark measure is used. Because there is no determinate value for Cuba, only rank correlations are appropriate for this measure. These correlations are .80 and .50 with the absolute and percentage CBR decline rates, respectively. The 1920-60 percentage increase in school enrollment is virtually unrelated to natality decline rates. Product-moment correlations are .152 and −.085, while the rank correlations are .314 and .086. Unfortunately, the very low number of cases makes statistical significance almost impossible, but increases in school enrollment seem to be related to CBR decline rates if the better (benchmark) measure is used.

With urbanization, the results are more encouraging. The percentage change in proportion urban from 1930 to 1960 is correlated .744 and .814 with the CBR decline rates (rank correlations are .881 and .857). These figures are significant at the 5 percent level. The absolute change in proportion urban yields correlations of .840 and .806 (rank correlations of .714 and .810; each is significant at the 5 percent level).

The gross domestic product indicator gives mildly supportive results. Percent change in GDP correlates .217 and .376 with absolute and percent natality decline rates respectively (rank correlation: 0 and .133); comparable figures for absolute GDP change are higher: .329 and .527 (rank correlations: .167 and .333).

The general impression is one of modest support for the hypothesis. Even the results obtained with the national product data do not really refute the hypothesis and the correlations are of the proper sign, although their magnitudes are negligible considering the sample size.

The acceleration in development indicators over time. The rate of change in development measures, like mortality indicators, has tended to increase over time, and there is a pronounced association of rapid development and natality reduction across time periods. This point is illustrated with changes in school enrollment ratio and the percentage of the population said to be urban. Relatively large increases have been underlined for emphasis in both parts of Table 6-8. Their concentration in more recent periods is quite obvious.

Historical data on national product are not sufficiently available to allow a direct demonstration of acceleration of increases in Latin America. However, one can infer from what is available that recent rises in national product per capita have been relatively great, and in some cases unprecedented. For instance, by 1950 only two of the nine countries listed in Table 6-7, part III had gross domestic products of over $450 per person (1963 U.S. dollars), these being Argentina and Uruguay. Furthermore, even in these countries the previous rates of improvement in national product were probably small; a series estimated by the World Bank (International Bank, 1970) indicates that between 1929 and 1950 the gross national product per capita in Argentina actually declined, and from 1913 to 1950 the rise was only 13.7 percent. By 1965 two other countries, Puerto Rico and Trinidad and Tobago, had attained GDPs of over $700 per person, and two more, Jamaica and Panama, had surpassed $450. Table 6-7, part III, shows that during 1950-65 three of the nine countries in the table had increases in per capita GDP of over 95 percent, and the median is 43.6 percent. These changes are almost certainly large relative to earlier periods in Latin

Table 6-7
Rates of Development and Natality Decline

Part I: School Enrollment and Natality

| Country | Rate of Increase in School Enrollment and Rank | | | | Annual Rate of Decline in the Crude Birth Rate (Postwar) | | | |
| | Years to Move from 1000 to 1500 Enrollment Ratio | | 1920-60 % Increase in Enrollment Ratio | | | | | |
	Years	Rank	Percent	Rank	Absolute	Rank	Percent	Rank
Chile	37	4	43.8	6	.683	3	2.10	2
Costa Rica	18	2	135.9	3	1.133	1	2.78	1
Cuba	37[a,c]	5	72.5	5	.327	6	1.12	5
El Salvador[a]	10[b]	1	195.3	1	.686	2	1.49	3
Guatemala[a]	d	N.A.	88.6	4	.500	4	1.02	6
Panama[a]	24	3	188.2	2	.438	5	1.13	4

PART II: Urbanization and Natality

| Country | Increase in Proportion Urban, 1930-1960 | | Change in Percentage Urban, 1930-1960 | | Annual Rate of Decline in the Crude Birth Rate (post-war) | | | |
	%	Rank	Change	Rank	Absolute	Rank	Percent	Rank
Chile	42.4	5	19.2	1	.683	4	2.10	4
Costa Rica	78.6	2	15.1	4	1.133	1	2.78	2
Cuba	12.2	8	5.7	7	.327	8	1.17	6
Guyana[a]	19.4	7	4.7	8	.448	6	1.10	8
Jamaica	74.9	3	12.5	5	.606	5	1.61	5
Panama[a]	37.9	6	11.4	6	.438	7	1.13	7
Puerto Rico	61.9	4	16.9	3	.900	3	2.70	3
Trinidad and Tobago	83.3	1	18.0	2	.938	2	3.18	1

Part III: Gross Domestic Product (GDP) and Natality

County	Increase in GDP per Capita, 1950-1965		Change in GDP per Capita, 1950-1965		Annual Rate of Decline in the Crude Birth Rate			
	%	Rank	Change	Rank	Absolute	Rank	Percent	Rank
Chile	24.7	9	62	9	.683	5	2.10	4
Costa Rica	27.1	8	79	6	1.133	1	2.78	2
El Salvador	36.4	6	64	8	.686	4	1.49	6
Guatemala[a]	41.4	5	88	5	.500	7	1.02	9
Guyana[a]	34.7	7	77	7	.448	8	1.10	8
Jamaica	129.7	2	262	3	.606	6	1.61	5
Panama[a]	50.8	4	159	4	.438	9	1.13	7
Puerto Rico	159.2	1	659	1	.900	3	2.70	3
Trinidad and Tobago	95.3	3	347	2	.938	2	3.18	1

[a]Possible natality decline.

[b]The datum for 1965 is 1497; this was taken to be equivalent to 1500.

[c]The initial datum for Cuba was 1135 in 1920.

[d]1000 was not attained until the 1960s; 1500 has not been recorded in available data; the rankings of natality decline were reordered to exclude Guatemala when calculating rank correlations with this variable.

Note: Throughout the table, natality decline rates used are taken from Table 6-3. Chilean and Cuban rates are for the post-World-War-II period. School enrollment data are from Banks (1971), and are defined as the total of primary and secondary students per 10,000 population. Except as noted below, urbanization data are from United Nations *Demographic Yearbooks*. The 1930 datum for Jamaica was constructed by projecting backwards the 1960 observation from Davis (1969) on the basis of percentage change in the population of St. Andrews and Kingston parishes (the predominant urban center). For Guyana and Trinidad and Tobago, the 1960 data are from Davis (1969). Gross domestic products are in 1963 U.S. dollars and are from United Nations *Statistical Yearbooks*, supplemented by Banks (1971).

Table 6-8

Changes in Primary and Secondary School Enrollment Per 10,000 Population and Percentage of the Population Defined as Urban, Countries with Natality Decline

PART I: School Enrollment

Country	Changes in the School Enrollment Ratio during:				
	1913-25	1925-35	1935-46	1946-55	1955-65
Argentina	128	273	−61	89	1,887
Chile	180	−176	272	115	227
Costa Rica	35	299	−375	990	529
Cuba	N.A.	158	60	−76	561
El Salvador[a]	−58	76	213	346	494
Guatemala[a]	−22	76	−61	189	335
Panama[a]	596	63	361	419	157
Uruguay	−138	158	−94	157	487

PART II: Urbanization

Country	Changes in Proportion of the Population Defined as Urban in the Decade Beginning with the Year:			
	1930	1940	1950	1960
Argentina	N.A.	N.A.	8.7	3.5
Chile	2.8	6.0	10.4	11.3
Costa Rica	N.A.	N.A.	.8	1.4
Cuba	1.9	2.0	1.8	3.0
El Salvador[a]	N.A.	N.A.	1.8	.1
Guatemala[a]	N.A.	N.A.	5.8	5.9
Guyana	2.1	1.6	1.0	.3
Jamaica	2.2	6.6	6.4	8.9
Panama[a]	3.7	2.2	5.5	6.2
Puerto Rico	3.0	10.2	3.7	14.0
Trinidad and Tobago	1.0	3.3	13.7	13.7
Uruguay	N.A.	N.A.	15.4	12.2

[a]Possible natality decline.

Note: School enrollment ratios are from Banks (1971) (see note to Table 6-7); increases of over 300 per time period are underlined. All Guatemalan data are from Davis (1969); otherwise the 1930-60 urbanization data are as in Table 6-7. The 1940 data are from official sources given in the United Nations *Demographic Yearbooks*, as are 1950 data. 1960 data are from *Demographic Yearbooks* (except for Costa Rica, Trinidad-Tobago, Uruguay and Guatemala, which are from Davis (1969), and are projections based on 1969 information.

America, and it should be noted that these are per capita rates calculated on the basis of rapidly growing populations. Recent increases in absolute national product would be much more dramatic.

Conclusion: hypothesis 2b. The data confirm a mild tendency for countries with rapid increases in development measures to have fast natality declines and vice versa; hypothesis 2b does receive some support in its original form. As with hypothesis 2a, there is a strong indication that the hypothesis would hold if applied over time rather than to countries (whose periods of development span different periods). There are presumably forces that have allowed more rapid development (as measured) in the more recent past. This is quite understandable, in view of the efforts of many governments in Latin America, and other developing regions, to make "progress" in terms of these indicators and to utilize aspects of technology and social and economic organization borrowed from other societies to attain this end. Whether the acceleration in socioeconomic change has been responsible, in whole or in part, for the acceleration in natality decline cannot be determined from these data.

Conclusion: Predicting Differential
Rates of Natality Decline

The most perplexing aspect of the findings is the failure of rate of mortality decline to predict rate of natality decline, while other development indicators prove to be at least moderately successful in this task. Certainly there is considerable measurement error in rates of mortality decline, but there is no reason to believe that other development indicators would not be similarly afflicted. Some have argued that mortality is no longer related to socioeconomic development. As suggested by the evaluation of hypothesis 3 (below), this does not seem to hold up under scrutiny: the *levels* of mortality are inversely related to *levels* of development indicators. I would offer the alternative interpretation, however, that the *rate* at which mortality can be reduced *is* fairly well determined by the available level of death control technology upon which all developing nations can draw. Indeed, the rate of mortality decline in the Latin American region has been so great since 1930 that it is hard to imagine how there could be much variance (in rate of decline); in fact there *is* very little variance, except that due to ceiling-floor effects, and hypothesis 2a presumably fails for this reason.

On the other hand, it is gratifying that rates of change in measures of development do predict rates of change in natality Although the level of predictability is less than might have been desired, the results are quite encouraging, in view of the dubious reliability of much of the data and the fact that it is not always possible to observe really comparable segments of development in different countries.

An important supplementary finding has also been made: rates of development and mortality and natality have all tended to accelerate over time. In this way, rates of change have been temporally associated (with major mortality reductions leading natality declines by about thirty years). Unless this trend is an extraordinary fluke, there is an excellent chance that future natality declines (in countries that have not yet begun to reduce birth rates) will be very rapid. From a practical standpoint, this is a very important consideration.

Hypothesis 3: Predicting the Occurrence of Natality Decline

Overview

Hypothesis 3 states that countries with advanced development and low mortality are most likely to reduce natality. In a sense, hypothesis 3 is more important than any of the others considered in this chapter, although the same theoretical relationships are involved in the derivation of hypotheses 1a-1c, 2a, and 2b. Hypothesis 3 has superior practical importance because it examines the accuracy with which natality decline can be predicted, rather than the rate at which it proceeds, assuming it begins. This is critical to the demographic future of Latin America, since many countries do not at this time have documented natality reductions and almost all are experiencing rapid population growth. Theoretically, it is more desirable to be able to predict that fundamental social change will soon lead to a natality decline than to deal with natality decline after it is under way and it is already clear that social change is having its presumed effect.

Hypothesis 3 is also relatively easy to test. First, its predictions cover every country in the region, since in principle each has either had or not had natality decline. This creates a larger sample. Second, long time series of data are not necessary to test the hypothesis; one need only know whether and about when natality decline has occurred and the levels of development and mortality indicators preceding that time.

Methods

It should be noted that hypothesis 3 does *not* assert that every country begins natality decline at similar levels of development or mortality—it is not a threshold hypothesis in the strict sense. Rather the hypothesis states that, among countries that have not experienced natality decline, those with relatively high levels of development and low mortality *at a given time* will be more likely than others to begin natality decline earlier. The actual levels of development or mortality at which natality decline begins may change over time without refuting the hypothesis.

Our prior investigation revealed that a useful distinction could be made between Latin American countries beginning natality decline well before World

War II and those that have begun only after World War II. Because of the great time separating these two phases of natality decline, hypothesis 3 is tested for its applicability to each period. First we ascertain whether countries with early natality declines had relatively high levels of development and low mortality at the appropriate time; then we consider whether countries recently beginning natality decline could have been predicted on the basis of high development and low mortality levels in the immediate post-World-War-II ("postwar") period.

Results: Predicting Early Natality Declines

Natality data for this period consist mainly of five-year birth rates estimated by Collver (1965) and, for Uruguay, Rothman (1969), supplemented by information for some Caribbean areas from United Nations *Demographic Yearbooks* (see Appendix, Table A-4). These data identify three countries with steady crude birth rate declines equal to or greater than 30 percent between 1895-99 and 1940-44 (the latter period showing no perceptible war effects in any): Argentina, Cuba, and Uruguay. Chile's crude birth rates fall 14.7 percent during this period, but subsequently recover and then decline again in earnest in the late 1950s. No other country shows any pattern of steady natality decline in the pre-World-War-II era. While the data upon which these observations are based may not always be of the highest quality, I am assuming that a major natality decline would be detectable; for discussion of the basic data see Collver (1965), Rothman (1969) and, for certain Caribbean areas, United Nations *Demographic Yearbooks*. Thus we have three clear cases of early natality decline—Argentina, Cuba, and Uruguay—and one dubious case, Chile.

Table 6-9 shows the results of contrasting these countries with the remaining countries of the region in terms of widely recognized development and mortality indicators. The coefficient of separation is defined as the percent of all possible paired comparisons between the countries above the dashed line and those below in which the former have lower mortality or higher levels of other development measures. Even counting Chile as part of the natality-declining group, there is considerable support for hypothesis 3. It should also be noted that each coefficient reflects the explanatory power of only one of the independent variables, and that their combined power would be greater. For instance, while British Caribbean areas had levels of school enrollment that seem "too high," these same countries have unusually low levels of urbanization. Thus their lack of early natality decline is much more consistent with proposition 1 when the indicators are considered together. With Chile eliminated from the analysis (as a dubious case of minor natality decline) most coefficients of separation increase and the contrast between countries above and below the dashed line is enhanced.

Had a social scientist used transition theory notions to try to choose the countries most likely to have early natality declines on the basis of early

Table 6-9

Mortality and Development: Comparison of Countries Having Early Natality Declines with Others in Latin America

Country	Expectation of Life at Birth (e_0)		CDR 1920-24	School Enrollment per 10,000 Population		% in Cities of 50,000+ 1910	% Urban 1930
	c.1900	c.1920		1910	1920		
Argentina	37.4 (1895)	48.3 (1914)	14.0	970	1,401	26.4	52.7+
Chile	28.7[a]	30.5[a]	31.3[a]	1,099[a]	1,199[a]	17.0[a]	45.5[a]
Cuba	N.A.	N.A.	19.3	N.A.	1,138	26.6	46.9
Uruguay	52.4 (1908)	52.4 (1908)	11.5	1,060	878	30.3	N.A.
Brazil	29.4	32.0	N.A.	284	473	N.A.	27.1
Colombia	N.A.	32.0	23.7	N.A.	N.A.	3.8	N.A.
Costa Rica	N.A.	N.A.	25.2	708	807	0	19.2
Dominican Republic	26.1 (1930)[b]	26.1 (1930)[b]	N.A.	N.A.	1,053	N.A.	17.4
Ecuador	N.A.	N.A.	28.9	446	603	13.3	N.A.
El Salvador	28.7 (1930)[b]	28.7 (1930)[b]	N.A.	520	N.A.	N.A.	N.A.
Guatemala	24.0	25.5	33.7	N.A.	448	8.2	26.7
Guyana	N.A.	34.8 (1920-22)	27.7	N.A.	N.A.	19.4	24.2
Haiti	N.A.	N.A.	N.A.	N.A.	N.A.	5.3	N.A.
Honduras	N.A.	N.A.	N.A.	705	468	0	17.6
Jamaica	N.A.	37.0 (1920-22)	23.4	1,510	1,511	6.9	16.7
Mexico	25.3	34.0	28.4	572	466	6.9	33.5

Nicaragua	N.A.	24.3	N.A.	363	610	0	35.7
Panama	N.A.	N.A.	17.3	367	626	0	30.1
Paraguay	26.2	31.0	N.A.	709	1,144	11.9	N.A.
Peru	N.A.	N.A.	N.A.	351	387	3.3	23.9
Puerto Rico	N.A.	N.A.	21.0	1,086	1,423	0	27.3
Trinidad and Tobago	37.7 (1900-03)	38.8 (1920-22)	21.6	1,345	1,251	18.0	21.6
Venezuela	N.A.	31.3	26.0	N.A.	87	3.6	21.6
Coefficient of Separation	85.7%	77.8%	75.0%	79.5%	76.7%	96.9%	100.0%
Coefficient of Separation (excluding Chile)[a]	92.9%	100.0%	97.0%	76.9%	75.6%	100.0%	100.0%

[a]Chile has a partial natality decline during this period; the first coefficients of separation show the results of including Chile among natality-declining areas; the second set shows the results of excluding Chile from all calculations.

[b]The 1930 data are the earliest available; under the assumption that e_0 tends to increase in the long run, the 1900 and 1920 figures were taken to be somewhat less.

Note: Countries above the dashed line are those with early natality declines; those below the dashed line are without such declines—Bolivia is excluded for lack of data. The coefficient of separation is the percent of possible paired comparisons in which a country above the dashed line had lower mortality or higher development levels than a country below the line. The CDR is the crude death rate (per 1000 population per year).

Sources: The e_0 data are from Arriaga (1968), except for Argentina and Uruguay, which are from Rothman (1969), and Guyana, Jamaica, Puerto Rico, and Trinidad and Tobago (United Nations Demographic Yearbooks). CDR data are from Collver (1965), except for Uruguay (Rothman, 1969), and Guyana, Jamaica, Puerto Rico, and Trinidad and Tobago (United Nations Demographic Yearbook, 1951—these data are for the years 1921-25). School enrollment data are from Banks (1971). Percent of population in cities of 50,000 or more inhabitants is from Banks (1971), except for Jamaica and Puerto Rico (United Nations Demographic Yearbooks). Percent of the population that is urban is from United Nations Demographic Yearbooks, with some definitional adjustments based on discrepancies between 1950 official data and estimates for that year made by Davis (1969). The datum for Argentina in this column (52.7) is actually for 1914, with the "+" appended to indicate the assumption that by 1930 the true proportion urban had increased. Linear interpolation was sometimes used to make the e_0 and % urban data more comparable across countries when observations were not available for exactly the proper years.

twentieth century data, he would probably have named Argentina, Cuba, and Uruguay as the most obvious cases. He might well have been puzzled about the position of Chile, as we still are, but at worst he would have identified three of four countries, and that is a rather high accomplishment for a social science theory. Urbanization and mortality measures clearly differentiate the Argentina-Cuba-Uruguay group from almost all other countries. School enrollment discriminates well except for some of the Caribbean nations and (oddly) Paraguay. The level of predictability shown by hypothesis 3 is quite high given any realistic standards.

Results: Predicting Postwar
Natality Declines

The determination of natality trends since World War II rests upon two basic data sources. Of the remaining Latin American countries (those without early natality declines), nine had birth registration deemed "complete" by the United Nations in 1969, while eleven did not. For those lacking complete registration five-year crude birth rate estimates are available (United Nations, 1969, and United Nations *Demographic Yearbook*, 1970).

Given that the generation of reliable statistical data is itself associated with development, it is not surprising that almost half of the countries with complete registration show evidence of substantial natality decline. This very fact lends support to hypothesis 3. Examining the annual data for the postwar period, we find that Costa Rica, Jamaica, Puerto Rico, and Trinidad-Tobago have crude birth rate declines of over 20 percent from the postwar three-year peak. Costa Rica and Puerto Rico also have age-standardized data confirming the trend. In contrast, of the countries with reliable annual natality data only Mexico shows virtually no indication of a decline.

Four countries with annual registration data said to be complete show possible natality declines. From the maximum three-year to most recent observations the crude birth rates of El Salvador, Guatemala, and Guyana decline by about 18, 20 and 17 percent respectively. El Salvador and Guyana exhibit a reasonably consistent downward pattern, but Guatemala does not (see Appendix, Table A-4). More important, none of these countries has ever reached a CBR of 35 or less, as our definition of "decline" demands. Unfortunately the CBR can have rather large fluctuations at high absolute levels; furthermore, these countries lack adequate refined natality measures needed for verification of the trend. These cases have been classed as "possible" declines and treated separately in Table 6-10. Panama has exhibited a fairly steady drop in its CBR to about 35 and the trend is confirmed by standardized data, but the low magnitude of the decline (13 percent) prompted its inclusion in the doubtful category.

For the remaining eleven countries the United Nations provides crude birth rate estimates that it considers reliable (United Nations, 1969, and *Demographic Yearbook*, 1969:12). Unfortunately these are five-year data and cannot be directly compared with the annual data used above. If we accept the criterion of a 15 percent decline in the CBR to 35 or lower to identify natality reduction, we must arrive at a comparable figure for five-year rates. Examination of annual data indicated that countries with rapid natality declines, e.g., El Salvador and Jamaica, could exhibit 15 percent reductions in annual rates but have declines of as little as 10 percent after aggregating the data into five-year periods. In view of this problem it is gratifying that only Brazil, of the remaining countries, has an estimated natality decline that approaches this level—Brazil's decline is not quite 10 percent, and the last estimated CBR is about 38 (see Appendix). Brazil is added to the list of doubtful cases for this reason, while the other countries are considered to have had no natality decline.

Table 6-10 contrasts those countries with confirmed natality declines beginning since World War II with those where no declines have occurred.[b] The data shown are *circa* 1950 so as to test the ability to predict *subsequent* natality decline. In general the coefficients of separation show support for the proposition. The degree of support varies, however, and there are some special features of the data that require closer examination.

Mortality ties with literacy as the best predictor of natality trends. This is favorable to transition theory, which makes mortality decline a fundamental cause of natality decline. The other development variables fare almost as well, with the single exception of urbanization.

The proportion of the population listed as "urban" (Davis, 1969) is the only conspicuously poor predictor of natality decline, operating at chance level. This is a reversal of results obtained for the pre-World-War-II period. To a large extent, this is due to the relatively low urbanization levels in the three ex-British colonies. These data may be misleading.

Although Davis attempts to correct some of the more obvious problems with cross-national differences in the definition of urban, he uses national definitions "unless there is reason to believe it is a clear distortion" (Davis, 1969:11). In Jamaica and Trinidad and Tobago (and Guyana), the definition of urban is effectively limited to a few cities and towns—in Guyana all the urban population is in two cities, and in Jamaica over 83 percent of the urban population in 1950 was in one metropolitan area. In the Latin American countries affected by Iberian influence, the definition of "urban" tends to be much more liberal, taking in administrative centers of "municipios" with a minimal population—i.e., the minimal population often applied to the whole municipio—or with "urban" characteristics such as streetlights (Davis, 1969:285-92).

This definitional problem can be partly eliminated by examining only large

---

[b]The list of countries with possible and confirmed natality declines is in substantial agreement with that determined independently by the Population Council (1974), except that the Council places Colombia among the "possibles," while omitting Panama.

Table 6-10

Mortality and Development: Comparison of Countries Having Recent Natality Declines with Other, High Natality Countries in Latin America (Data are *circa* 1950)

Country	e_0	% Enrolled in School Ages 5-19	% Urban	% Literate Ages 15 and Over	Telephones per 100,000 Population	GDP per Capita	% in Cities 100,000
Costa Rica	55.5	37	33.3	79.4	1,161	245	17.4
Jamaica	56.4	50	22.8	74.9	1,043	202	19.0
Puerto Rico	60.5	58	40.5	73.3	1,843	361	33.3
Trinidad and Tobago	57.0	66	25.9	73.9	2,488	364	0
Bolivia	43.1	20	20.4	32.1	324	123	9.9
Colombia	48.5	22	37.0	62.3	793	192	17.4
Dominican Republic	43.7	31	23.8	42.9	300	126	8.5
Ecuador	47.9	32	28.5	55.7	275	124	14.6
Haiti	39.4	16	12.2	10.5	112	94	4.3
Honduras	42.7	16	17.7	35.2	392	176	0
Mexico	47.6	30	42.6	56.8	1,105	258	15.1
Nicaragua	40.1	22	34.9	38.4	292	164	10.3
Paraguay	45.8	40	32.9	65.8	376	150	16.3
Peru	39.9	34	35.5	51.8	555	116	11.4
Venezuela	52.6	30	45.2	52.2	1,352	462	20.3
Coefficient of Separation	100.0%	97.7%	50.5%	100.0%	93.2%	81.8%	70.5%

Brazil[a]	43.0	22	36.1	49.4	1,057	148	17.5
El Salvador[a]	47.2	23	36.5	40.4	396	184	8.7
Guatemala[a]	40.7	17	24.9	29.4	196	204	10.5
Guyana[a]	53.9	58	27.9	76.0	N.A.	222	0
Panama[a]	50.2	46	36.0	69.9	1,668	313	15.9

[a]Countries with uncertain natality trends, excluded from coefficients of separation (see text).

Sources: The expectation of life at birth (e_0) is from Arriaga (1968) except as noted in Table 6-9. Interpolation was used where no datum was available for the exact year 1950. School Enrollment figures represent the enrollment in primary and secondary schools (times 100) divided by the population between the ages of 5 and 19; these are from UNESCO *Statistical Yearbooks*; the datum for Haiti is for 1952 and that for Nicaragua is for 1951. Urbanization data are from Davis (1969). Literacy data are from United Nations *Demographic Yearbooks* and are for the population fifteen years of age and over, except for Honduras (10 and over), Mexico (6 and over), and Peru (17 and over); the data for Guyana, Jamaica, and Trinidad and Tobago are for 1946, for Colombia, 1951; and for Peru, the datum is the average of the observations for 1940 and 1961. Information on the number of telephones per 100,000 population is from Banks (1971), except for Jamaica, Puerto Rico, and Trinidad and Tobago, which were calculated from the number of telephones in service (United Nations *Statistical Yearbooks*) and estimated midyear populations (United Nations *Demographic Yearbooks*). Percentage of the population in cities of 100,000 or more inhabitants is from Davis (1969).

cities. If the proportion of the population in cities of 100,000 or more people is used as the urbanization measure, the ex-British colonies no longer appear more rural than other countries with recent natality declines, and results improve as shown in the last column of Table 6-10. This measure was chosen post hoc, however, and is not a "clean" test of the hypothesis.

Two countries deserve special mention because of their anomalous character-istics—Mexico and Venezuela exhibit high enough values on most mortality-development variables to be in the natality-declining group. A possible reason for this discrepancy is discussed in terms of hypotheses 4a and 4b below; however, my first reaction would be to predict that these two countries (along with Brazil, which has made rapid progress since 1950) will be the next to exhibit identifiable reductions in the birth rate. The United Nations (1969, and *Demographic Yearbook*, 1970) already indicates about a 10 percent decline in the Brazilian crude birth rate.

Epilogue: Indications of 1970
Census Data

At the time of the original draft of this manuscript data from the 1970 round of Latin American censuses had only begun to trickle out. Since these raw data require considerable analysis and refinement for our purposes, they could not add greatly to information available from other sources, nor could they be very helpful in determining doubtful cases. During the past two years, however, research reports have appeared that do lend support to the present theoretical framework. Whereas before 1970 confirmed natality declines had occurred in several smaller nations of the region (in addition to the four larger nations that had begun natality decline much earlier), I could only anticipate and forecast a reduction in birth rates in three of the largest countries; Brazil, Mexico, and Venezuela. It was clear that the argument would rest heavily on these cases, and now there are indications that the predictions are being realized.

First we encounter Brazil, previously placed in the doubtful category for natality trends as a result of an estimated 10 percent CBR reduction (United Nations, 1969). Brazil did not present a contradiction in terms of its develop-ment circa 1950 (Table 6-10) because much of its modernization has been very recent; any reasonable lag time would postpone the prediction of natality decline. Nevertheless its late-1960s levels of development place it near the top of the group of nations without confirmed natality decline, making it a crucial theoretical test. (Even by 1962 this was largely the case—see Oechsli and Kirk, 1974.)

Reverse-survival calculations of Brazilian CBRs yield estimates of 46.3, 41.2, 40.3, 39.8, and 37.4 respectively for five-year periods beginning with 1945-50 and ending with 1965-70 (Oechsli and Adlahka, 1974: Table 6). This overall decline of 19.2 percent leaves Brazil in the doubtful category since the absolute level remains above 35, but it seems likely that the doubt is soon to be removed. These authors do contribute 2.3 points of the CBR decline to age structure change, but this still leaves a "true" reduction of 6.4 or 13.8 percent between 1945 and 1950 and 1965 and 1970.

Venezuela is probably the most conspicuous anomaly in Table 6-10, and the country most likely to have experienced natality decline recently. Although it has been argued that the influx of oil revenues and maldistribution of income causes distortion, Venezuela seems to be relatively developed regardless of the indicator chosen. Venezuela is a pivotal case for testing transition theory, and, until now at least, one of its most glaring failures.

Oechsli and Edmonston (1974) have calculated Venezuelan CBRs for census years and obtain rates of 42.4, 45.3, and 37.3 for 1950, 1961, and 1971. The 1961-71 decline of 17.3 percent leaves the nation as a borderline case because of the high level (above 35), but, as with Brazil, provides support for the transition theory predictions made prior to the analysis of the last census. Estimates of the total fertility rate for 1961, 6.67, and 1970, 5.62, scale down the estimated natality decline to 15.7 percent but confirm the trend (Oechsli and Edmonston, 1974).

Finally we encounter Mexico. Unlike Brazil and Venezuela, Mexico has long had reasonably accurate vital registration, and hence the analysis of census materials does not produce much new knowledge of natality. Only a very minor CBR reduction can be found in the 1972 rate of 43.4 (United Nations, 1974), compared with the five-year postwar peak of 46.5 (United Nations, 1969) in 1950-55. Mexico thus remains a problematic case for transition theory, although the experiences of Venezuela and Brazil give us reason to reserve judgment as the vital rates of the next few years are recorded.

Summary: Hypothesis 3

There is strong support for hypothesis 3. Predictions made on the basis of development-mortality levels *circa* 1950 are largely confirmed by the probable natality declines in Brazil and Venezuela, though not yet in Mexico. Natality decline, once confined to the four "old" nations of the region and some smaller republics, has at last become manifest in more populous countries, as the theory indicated.

Hypothesis 4

Overview

This hypothesis goes beyond the usual content of the theory of the demographic transition, and represents an extension of the idea that certain aspects of the predevelopment culture (openness and exposure to modernizing influences) can affect the date at which natality decline begins. This effect is assumed to operate through development and mortality decline, although there may be a direct effect as well.

Measures

Following a rationale developed in Chapter 5, it was assumed that the openness-exposure dimensions of culture followed in decreasing order from countries that were extensions of southern Europe to those settled by Africans and/or East Indians, to mestizo countries, and finally to Amerindian populations. In effect, race is the measure of culture. Truly comparable quantitative data on racial composition would be extremely difficult to obtain, and the figures would probably be unreliable. Instead I have drawn upon sources described in Chapter 5 to form eight racial categories. These are displayed in Table 6-11. Openness-exposure is assumed to decrease from left to right and top to bottom. Countries that have had natality decline are noted, and the approximate dates at which their respective birth rates began to fall are shown in parentheses. These data are from Table 6-3.

Findings

There is a very obvious relationship in the expected direction between culture as measured by race and the occurrence of natality decline. All the countries in the first three groups, which are predominantly European, have had natality decline. Furthermore, the earliest natality reductions are in the first group, while the others are somewhat more recent—recall that birth rates in Cuba and Chile fell very early, but that the major portion of decline has been in the post-World-War-II period. Three out of four of the African-East Indian populations have had natality decline (one "possible"), all in the postwar era. Two of three countries in the next category, 5, have recently begun to reduce birth rates, but not enough to be unequivocal. There are only three instances of significant natality decline in categories 6, 7, and 8, none sufficient to be considered confirmed.

Cultural Background as a Cause of
Development and Mortality Decline

Although it is not a direct concern for the present research, it is clear that cultural openness-exposure is also related to the onset of major changes in development and mortality levels. There will be no special empirical considera-

Table 6-11

Countries of the Latin American Region by Racial Composition

(1) European	(2) European with Some African	(3) European with Some Amerindian
Argentina[a] (1875) Uruguay[a] (1895)	Cuba[a] (1905) Puerto Rico[a] (1949)	Chile[a] (1880) Costa Rica[a] (1955)
(4) African and/or East Indian	(5) Mixed with Substantial African	(6) Mainly Amerindian Minor European and African
Guyana[b] (1953) Haiti Jamaica[a] (1959) Trinidad and Tobago[a] (1954)	Brazil[c] (See note) Dominican Republic Panama[b] (1961)	Colombia Nicaragua

(7) Mestizo (Amerindian with Minor European)	(8) Amerindian
El Salvador[b] (1957) Honduras Mexico Peru Venezuela[c] (See note)	Bolivia Ecuador Guatemala[b] (1949) Paraguay

[a]This indicates a country that is experiencing or has experienced natality decline. The dates in parentheses behind these countries are the approximate years in which natality decline began. (However, natality declines in Argentina and Uruguay began earlier than indicated by the data series available.)

[b]Possible natality decline.

[c]Analysis of 1970 census materials suggests probable natality decline beginning recently.

Source: Chapter V, Section E, above.

tion of this effect, but relevant data can be found in the discussion of hypothesis 3, especially Tables 6-9 and 6-10. The countries that experience early natality decline are also the ones to achieve a greater degree of development and mortality control. In either case, cultural background is associated with the timing of demographic change.

In the most recent period, development and mortality decline have spread to the mestizo and Amerindian countries. Because of the very rapid pace of change since World War II, some of these (notably Mexico and Venezuela) have surpassed some countries in categories 1-4 in certain respects. This confirms the view expressed above that cultural background can facilitate (or delay) socio-

118

demographic change but does not represent a permanent advantage or disadvantage. It is to be hoped that natality decline will take hold in the mestizo and Amerindian countries, just as development and mortality decline have already done.

The Direct Effect of Cultural
Background upon Natality

If cultural background (openness-exposure to modernizing influences) affects natality independently, as well as through development and mortality, then the residuals of birth rates, that portion not explained by other variables in the system, should be related to the cultural categories already established. Table 6-12 shows the mean of these natality residuals for each five-year period since 1950 by racial-cultural groups.

The residuals are indeed low for groups 1, 2, and 4; however, there is no particular progression across these categories. Groups 6 and 7 do have high residuals, but this does not apply to the most overwhelmingly Amerindian countries of group 8.

Table 6-12 suggests that, while controlling for other independent variables does obscure its impact, culture still seems to have a direct effect upon natality. However, an examination of the results also shows that the effect seems to be nonadditive, as previously suggested. As presently measured, the cultural characteristics of a country are unaltered over time, in contrast to other

Table 6-12
Mean Residuals of the Regression Analysis of the Age-Sex Standardized Birth Rate According to Cultural Background (Openness-Exposure to Modernizing Influences) Indexed by Racial Composition

Period	(1)	(2)	(3)	(4)	(5)	(6)	(7)	(8)
				Cultural Racial Categories[a]				
1950-54	−10.2	−6.3	+3.7	−6.5	−2.2	−.5	+1.0	−1.0
1955-59	−3.9	−2.5	+7.0	−4.1	+2.8	+3.6	+3.4	+.5
1960-64	−1.9	−4.3	+.8	−1.6	+5.0	+3.8	+5.8	+2.7
1965-69	−2.0	−2.4	−3.2	−1.7	−.3	+1.9	+5.7	−2.9

[a](1) European; (2) European with some African; (3) European with some Amerindian; (4) African and/or East Indian; (5) Mixed with substantial African; (6) Mainly Amerindian with minor European and African; (7) Mestizo (Amerindian with minor European); (8) Amerindian.

Note: Countries in each cultural-racial category can be found in Table 6-11. For an explanation of the age-sex standardized birth rate, see Chapter 5. The regression analysis is presented in the next chapter.

independent variables, but its impact on social and demographic variables does change. This is one of the main reasons why this factor was not included in the regression equation itself.

Since culture does seem to have some direct effect on natality, there must be a mechanism through which this operates without involving development and mortality. The measure of cultural background is far too broad to identify the nature of this relationship, but two related facets of culture do seem to be important: family structure and sex roles.

Southern European countries, which provided most of the European immigrants to Latin` America, subscribed to sex roles that can only be described as exceptionally chauvanistic, with very different standards of sexual behavior for men and women and a strong ideal of male dominance—these persisted in southern Europe even after a certain amount of change had occurred in other European societies. On the other hand, nuclear families are and were quite stable and the kinship system exerted rather strict controls over sexual behavior. The net result seems to have been late marriage and early reduction of natality. (See Goode, 1961; Heer, 1964; and Stycos, 1968.)

In many (predominantly mestizo) countries of Latin America the chauvanism of southern Europe becomes what is popularly called "machismo." Having adopted some of the same sexual ideals of southern Europe, these countries seem to lack the social controls necessary to contain the resulting behavior. In addition, the social structure of the indigenous society has been disrupted—note that natality residuals are lower in countries that are most clearly Amerindian; possibly these have maintained better social controls (see Heer, 1964). More commonly, very high illegitimacy and high fertility at young ages have been the consequences. In a society in which many births are illegitimate and even married men may have few obligations to their wives, birth control could be difficult to institute. This could be one important reason why the non-European, nonblack populations seem to persist longer at high natality. It is also interesting that abortion is fairly common in Latin America (Requena, 1968). This is a female method of birth limitation that can be practiced without the cooperation of the male or without interfering with his sexual desires.

The African-East Indian countries show a totally different pattern. Here illegitimacy is also exceedingly common but the southern European pattern of sex roles is absent. This creates two separate reasons to expect moderate natality. First, the sexual unions are often so unstable that natality is limited by that very fact. Second, women in these countries are more free (and less inhibited) to engage in many activities, including the control of natality.

The above must be regarded as a speculative and incomplete argument. Nevertheless, the data are suggestive. Cultural background could have the observed direct effect on natality by operating through family structure and sex roles. If so, it would be optimal if these things could be measured directly and in such a way as to reflect changes over time. For the present analysis, this does not seem to be very feasible, and so this task must be reserved for future research. Nevertheless, the data indicate that the relationships of the other independent variables with natality should not be greatly or permanently disturbed by this factor. The main effect of culture operates through variables in the system, and its remaining direct effect seems to be reduced with development (note that for most cultural groups, especially the more developed ones, the natality residuals tend to moderate in the last period).

Conclusions: Hypotheses 1-4

This chapter has attempted to test some of the basic ideas of transition theory in the form of specific hypotheses (1-3). Certain problems have been avoided by concentrating on the Latin American region, and hypothesis 4 carries this cultural factor further by examining certain differences among cultural-racial categories within the region.

There is every indication that the basic causal forces of the demographic transition are operating in the Latin American region. Natality has declined in many countries, and by and large it has declined in the more likely places, as predicted by transition theory. Furthermore, the accelerating rates of change in development indicators and mortality decline have been followed by increasingly rapid rates of natality decline in those countries where the birth rate has fallen significantly. Recalling Chapter 2, one would have to conclude that the theory works at least as well in Latin America as in Europe.

On the other hand, it is difficult to predict with any precision when natality decline will occur, or the rate at which it will proceed. Again, one would probably have had just as much trouble predicting events in Europe in the latter nineteenth century—that being the period when natality declines were beginning to become general, apparently a comparable period to the present-day Latin America. There seem to be four kinds of reasons for these predictive difficulties: measurement problems, questions of types of relationships, historical-cultural factors, and the causal incompleteness of models of natality determinants.

First, there are substantial problems in trying to measure "development." One does not know which aspect to measure, and if one simply seeks out the best predictor of natality it will not be known whether that aspect of development is truly more important or if its predictive capacity is a result of the selection process. Furthermore, even if one knew what to measure, the indicators of development might still be unreliable. Fortunately, the measurement of mortality has received much attention and the concept is relatively easy to define. Nevertheless, there still may be reliability problems, and there are distinct aspects of mortality (e.g., child and infant) that could have special effects on natality.

Second, even though it is fairly obvious that development and mortality have a powerful effect on natality, the form of the relationships and the lag times are not known. This can have a big impact on prediction. For instance, one would make much different predictions depending on whether a given causal relationship was linear or logarithmic or whether or not a specific "threshold effect" existed.

Third, there are certainly cultural differences even within the Latin American region that can modify relationships. Culture has been a major determinant of socioeconomic change, and thus works largely through other variables in the system; hence, its impact is controlled for the most part. Nevertheless, there seems to be an independent contribution of culture, operating through family structure and sex roles, that affects the timing of natality decline.

A more pervasive and obvious problem is created by historical forces that affect all countries, or virtually all, but vary over time. For instance, it was much easier to reduce mortality in 1960 than in 1900, other things being equal. While the level of mortality is still correlated with development, recent rates of mortality decline have little variance over countries, being extremely rapid almost everywhere except for obvious ceiling-floor effects.

Finally, natality is clearly affected by other factors in addition to long-run socioeconomic development and mortality levels. This fact is well known, and yet the expectation seems to persist that the most obvious transition theory arguments should explain almost all the variance in natality. Given that other variables can affect natality, especially in the short run, development and mortality should *not* be capable of extremely precise prediction; this is exactly what occurs.

This chapter confirms the existence of the causal relationships that form the basis of transition theory. In the next chapter, a combined cross-sectional longitudinal multivariate analysis will be used to attempt to deal with some of the problems outlined above. While these difficulties will not be overcome entirely, a much more complete and well-controlled test of the proposed model will be possible.

7

Multivariate Analysis of Recent Natality Trends (Hypotheses 5-9)

Introduction

This chapter presents the findings of a combined longitudinal-cross-sectional regression analysis of post-World-War-II natality trends. Hypotheses 5-9 are tested simultaneously by means of this methodology. All hypotheses received considerable support. Before these results are examined, however, the distinctive features of the current research should be noted.

First, longitudinal as well as cross-sectional differences in natality are dealt with. Even a casual examination of modern Latin American natality trends will demonstrate that they often appear incongruent with expectations based solely on the traditional transition theory model. The present model will be tested in view of these temporal changes, which would be excluded from a strictly cross-sectional analysis.

Second, new causal variables are operationalized simultaneously with independent variables suggested by transition theory. These extra factors include immediate mortality effects, as distinct from long-term effects, as well as the impacts of economic expansion and land availability ("family resources"). These variables are suggested by previous studies reviewed in Chapters 2 and 3. None is completely original but their operationalization along with the basic transition theory is novel.

Third, while linear relationships and assumed lag times are used in the primary analysis, there is some experimentation with different forms and lags. This process is somewhat limited by the availability and autocorrelation of certain variables, as discussed below. Since the hypotheses predict only monotonic relations, sometimes with lags, such experimentation, where it is possible, is theoretically permissible.

Fourth, the variables and measures were defined on theoretical and practical grounds before the analysis was performed. That is, there was no attempt to select variables or measures with strong predictive power after the fact. On the contrary, there is good reason to believe that the measures are still rather crude, as discussed in Chapter 5.

Finally, this analysis includes a cross-lag technique which partially controls reverse causation and autocorrelation of natality data. This method involves the inclusion of past natality level as a control variable. Some additional interpretation is required in dealing with cross-lag regression coefficients, however, so the results of the simple regression of natality on the independent variables will be

123

considered first. There are no meaningful differences in the implied direction of causal relationships produced by changing from a simple multilinear to the cross-lag method. Rather, the magnitudes of coefficients change and require reconsideration.

Findings of the Simple Multilinear Regression

General Predictability

For the period 1950-70, the independent variables together account statistically for 65.4 percent of the variance in the age-sex standardized birth rate (ASSBR) and 76.7 percent of the variance in the crude birth rate (CBR). By any standard, these are excellent results, statistically significant beyond the .01 level, even if one were to assume that effective sample size is only the number of countries (twenty-four).

The greater predictability of the CBR may be due to a number of factors. First the standardization technique may actually "overcorrect" for age structure distortions because of the particular age-specific natality pattern of many Latin American countries (see Chapter 5). This might introduce more distortion in the ASSBR than is present in the CBR. Furthermore, the ASSBR calculation requires data on the age-sex distribution of the population, and thus includes new possibilities for error. Finally, for whatever reasons, the ASSBR shows a greater tendency to rise over time than does the CBR. As will be seen below, the variables of the model that are designed to account for such phenomena seem somewhat less efficacious than other variables, possibly due to constraints and inaccuracies of measurement.

The slightly larger unstandardized coefficients obtained with the ASSBR reflect a greater range of values, especially at high levels, than displayed by the CBR. Some high-CBR countries in Latin America actually had relatively few women in the main reproductive years compared to the tremendous number of young girls who constitute the prospective future generations of mothers under the prevailing conditions of lowered mortality. In terms of theoretical implications, the ASSBR and CBR results are highly similar, and can usually be interpreted identically.

Hypothesis 5: The Development Measures

Socioeconomic development as measured by levels of living, urbanization, and education is assumed to be an overriding and long-term determinant of natality, and negatively related to it. Because of this, the observed relationships with natality should not depend greatly on controlling for the other variables in the system, and it might be permissible to examine both zero-order correlations as well as partial correlation and regression coefficients. It can be seen from Table 7-1 that the zero-order correlations with natality are in the expected negative direction, with urbanization attaining the highest absolute value for either the ASSBR or the CBR.

When the partial correlation and regression coefficients are examined, the predominance of urbanization is even more striking. The impact of the other variables now appears small and the partials of education with the ASSBR even reverse sign while remaining very small.

The very strong effects of urbanization must be regarded as a surprise. The variable does not appear to be very well measured (Davis, 1969:285-92), and it has been suggested (Hauser, 1968) that, regardless of measurement, urbanization experienced in such Third World countries is not a good indicator of social change. There are reasons, discussed below, to suspect that the partials presented in Table 7-1 overstate the singular importance of urbanization, but nonetheless it accounts for much of the variance in natality and appears to be a fundamental aspect of development, as it has been in the past.

On the other hand, it does not follow that levels of living and education are of little or no importance. All three development measures could be interpreted as aspects of the same phenomenon. If so, the relative impact of the three variables could be viewed as a result of the vagaries of measurement error. In fact, measures of product per capita and school enrollment tend to change rapidly and irregularly during this period. Urbanization changes much more linearly, and in this respect is similar to natality. This characteristic may enhance the partial regression and correlation coefficients attached to urbanization at the expense of the other development measures. Note also that cross-national differences in the definition of "urban" should have less effect when there are four observations over time for each country. This may explain why urbanization is a better predictor in the present analysis than in that of the previous chapter, which depended exclusively on cross-country comparisons. The usual tests show the partial relationships between urbanization and either natality measure to be highly significant. The other partial correlation and regression coefficients involving national product and school enrollment do not approach statistical significance. This holds true whether the sample size is taken to be only 24 (the number of countries) or 96 (the number of observations).

I have suggested as an alternative to the usual significance tests an examination of the unstandardized regression coefficients in light of the likely changes experienced during the transformation from a rural-agrarian to an urban-industrial society. For this purpose, it is of course necessary to estimate the probable range of variation for each of the three variables now being considered. Hypothetically, this range extends from the beginning of sustained socio-economic development to that level at which the norms and values governing

Table 7-1
Results of the Regression Analysis

Independent Variable	Dependent Variable					
	Age-Sex Standardized Birth Rate			Crude Birth Rate		
	Zero-Order Correlation	Regression Coefficient (standard error)[c]	Partial Correlation	Zero-Order Correlation	Regression Coefficient (standard error)[c]	Partial Correlation
Product per capita, lagged 7-1/2 yrs. before natality	−.564[a]	−.004 (.006)[c]	−.074	−.660[a]	−.004 (.005)[c]	−.091
Urbanization, lagged 10 yrs. before natality	−.687[a]	−.367[a] (.067)[c]	−.504[a]	−.720[a]	−.259[a] (.048)[c]	−.496[a]
School enrollment, lagged 7-1/2 yrs. before natality	−.451[a]	+.033 (.064)[c]	+.055	−.611[a]	−.020 (.046)[c]	−.047
Crude death rate, contemporaneous with natality	+.492	−.807[a] (.285)[c]	−.289[a]	+.641	−.545[a] (.204)[c]	−.273[a]
Expectation of life, lagged 10 yrs. before natality	−.633[a]	−.586[a] (.175)[c]	−.336[a]	−.778[a]	−.548[a] (.126)[c]	−.421[a]
Land availability, contemporaneous with natality	+.022	+2.673[a] (.726)[c]	+.365[a]	+.027	+1.918[a] (.522)[c]	+.365[a]
Economic expansion, contemporaneous with natality	+.346[a]	+21.944[b] (9.841)[c]	+.231[b]	+.310[a]	+16.837[a] (7.072)[c]	+.246[a]

[a]Statistically significant at the .01 level by a one-tailed t test using an assumed N of 96.
[b]Statistically significant at the .025 level by a one-tailed t test using an assumed N of 96.
[c]With $N = 96$.

Note: For exact definitions of variables, see Chapter 5. The significance levels are provided only as a guide, and it is not asserted that the tests on which they are based are applicable in this case. Observe that the zero-order correlations for the crude death rate with each dependent variable, although large, are not significant because of their signs.

childbearing are no longer affected by development.[a] The gross domestic product is probably the most difficult to deal with. Socioeconomic development seems to begin at about $200 per capita GDP (1963 U.S. dollars). However, it is more difficult to judge what level of GDP indicates a fully modern society. Some of the more advanced countries of the Latin American region already have GDPs per capita over $1000 and still have moderately high natality. However, allowance must be made for lagged effects yet to be felt, and there are nations elsewhere with GDPs at or below $1000 that are considered "developed." In Latin America it seems that the range of GDP likely to affect natality could run from about $200 to $1000 per capita, probably a broader range than in most other areas. The other development measures, urbanization and school enroll- ment, both have natural limits, and so their probable change is easier to estimate. In both instances they may begin at very low levels—as low as 10 percent. Under present conditions, these variables seem to be approaching "end" states of around 80 percent in the more developed Latin American nations. This would yield an expected change in each of 70 percent. Although the foregoing exercise can hardly be called more than educated guesswork, only rough approximations are needed to ascertain whether the model yields realistic predictions for the long term. Note that due to lagged effects which may be longer even than those hypothesized, and to the impact of other variables, both included and not included in the model, it does not follow that changes in these development variables will necessarily be translated into natality decline at once.

Using the above estimates, the regression coefficients presented in Table 7-1 imply an expected decrease of 3.5 points in the ASSBR and 3.1 in the CBR attributable to increases in levels of living (GDP). Urbanization would result in natality declines of 25.7 points in the ASSBR and 20.7 in the CBR. Finally, rising levels of education would appear to be associated with an *increase* of 2.3 in the ASSBR but a decrease of 1.6 in the CBR. Taken individually, these results demonstrate nothing more than the overwhelming power of urbanization. If all of these development indicators are considered as aspects of a closely interre- lated nexus, a practice which seems more reasonable, the combined development effects indicate a long-term drop of 26.9 in the ASSBR and 22.1 in the CBR. Considering the very high initial levels of natality in Latin America, these figures are plausible, although a bit high in view of the fact that natality-lowering effects of long-term mortality decline have not been considered (see hypothesis 7). It is quite conceivable, however, that the range of variation in one or more of these independent variables has been overestimated. In any case, the predicted development-related change in natality is tenable and realistic.

If it is true that the urbanization coefficients are overstated at the expense of

[a]Any assumed range of this type must be somewhat arbitrary. Following Janowitz (1971), the present analysis assumes that even minor socioeconomic development affects natality, though the effect may not show up for some time. Thus, the crucial range of development begins at or near the hypothetical condition of "zero" development (an agrarian society).

the other development variables, hypothesis 5 is strongly confirmed. Even without such a proviso, all of the zero-order correlations and five of the six partials are in the hypothesized direction.

Hypothesis 6: Short-term
Mortality Effects

Hypotheses 6 and 7 state, respectively, that the immediate effect of general mortality decline is to raise natality, while the long-range impact of improvements in child and infant survivorship are in the opposite direction. Therefore, only the partial coefficients are relevant to hypothesis 6, since only these allow the appropriate controls. Table 7-1 shows that the partial regression and correlation coefficients associated with the current crude death rate are indeed in the negative direction, indicating that a decline in mortality could be associated with an increase in natality. This relationship holds for both the ASSBR and the CBR.

With an assumed N of 96 all of the crucial coefficients are statistically significant at the 1 percent level. If the N were only 24, the partial coefficients would be significant at the 10 percent level with the ASSBR as dependent variable, and would be very close to this level with the CBR as dependent. The strength of the relationship, and the fact that it is even more apparent with the indirectly standardized ASSBR than the CBR, tends to refute the possibility that it is spuriously induced by age structure (see Chapter 5).

To utilize the alternative "significance" tests, the probable short-term fluctuation in the crude death rate must be estimated, and this of course involves defining "short-term." This is crucial, since eventually short-term changes become long-term and come to have the opposite effect on natality. The present model allows ten years for this process to occur. Although no exact answer is possible, this is a plausible period, since it would take that long for improvements in mortality to have a substantial impact on actual family size.

The data indicate that the crude death rate can decline about 5 points over ten years, provided the initial level is not already too low for further reduction. In the thirteen countries of the sample with CDRs over 15.0 in 1950-54, the mean decline over the next ten years is 5.0 and the median 5.1. This would suggest a corresponding temporary increase in natality of 4.0 in the ASSBR and 2.7 in the CBR. These figures are not really large, but they are certainly not negligible. Under appropriate circumstances, the model also allows economic expansion and/or the transfer of persons from the countryside to contribute to natality increase. Therefore, these calculations do not represent the maximum predicted amount by which natality could rise (or an impending decline offset).

Hypothesis 7: Long-term Effects
of Child and Infant Survival

Lagged survivorship, especially for infants and children, is hypothesized to be negatively related to natality. This is expected to be one of the major causes of long-term natality reduction—in this respect it resembles the development variables considered in hypothesis 5. For this reason, the relationship posited in hypothesis 7 should be observable in both the zero-order and partial coefficients linking expectation of life at age zero (e_0, the measurement of survivorship) and the birth rates. From Table 7-1, it can be seen that this is in fact the case. For the ASSBR, the correlations with e_0 are both in the proper direction. The zero-order coefficient is second only to that of urbanization in magnitude, and the partial is larger than all others except urbanization and land availability. For the CBR, the signs are again as expected, while the zero-order correlation with e_0 is the highest of any independent variable and the partial correlation is second only to urbanization.

A one-tailed t test with an assumed N of 96 shows all of the zero-order and partial coefficients linking e_0 and natality to be significant at the 1 percent level. With an N of 24, the partials would drop to the 5 percent level, while the zero-order correlations would remain at 1 percent.

The magnitude of the unstandardized regression coefficients also suggests an important role for child-infant survivorship as measured by e_0. During the course of socioeconomic development an improvement of forty years in e_0 is quite possible—from a level of about 25 (indicating an initial stationary population death rate of 40 per thousand population) to about 65 (currently observed in such countries as Argentina, Uruguay, and Puerto Rico). This would imply a decline of 23.5 points in the ASSBR and 21.9 in the CBR. This is both substantial and realistic.

Since socioeconomic development involves changes in levels of living, urbanization, and education as well as survivorship, some thought should be given to the combined effects of all these variables. The total natality reduction predicted by the posited changes in the development variables (see hypothesis 5) and survivorship would lead to an implied decline of 50.4 points in the ASSBR and 44.0 in the CBR. These figures clearly overstate the possibilities. But given the very high initial natality levels in most Latin American countries, a "complete" demographic transition could involve declines of 40 points in the ASSBR and perhaps 35 in the CBR. Thus the results produce estimates of long-term natality decline about 20 percent too high. We must conclude that our coefficients are somewhat, but not greatly, larger than those that could be sustained over a long-term natality decline. Presumably this is due to peculiarities of the period or the inclusion of cross-sectional variance or both.

Before concluding the discussion of mortality, it might be worth noting that both lagged e_0 and current crude death rate are highly correlated with the lagged development indicators. This can be seen from the table of intercorrelations in the Appendix. The findings give no reason to suppose that mortality is independent of socioeconomic change in Latin America, in contrast with Arriaga's conclusions (1970b). Mortality decline has been exceptionally rapid in the region, but the level of mortality is nevertheless associated with development indicators.

Hypothesis 8: Availability of Land

Hypothesis 8 predicts a positive association between the measure of availability of land (*ln* of land per 1000 rural persons weighted by the proportion of the population rural) and natality. It is difficult to take account of such factors as land quality, agricultural technology, land distribution, and land tenure and inheritance systems. Despite these limitations, the hypothesized relationship is readily observable. There was no particular reason to expect this relationship to be present in the zero-order correlation, but there was a small positive correlation between the land availability measure and each natality indicator. This could, however, be a spurious association brought about by the percentage of the population that is rural, which appears as a weighting factor. Therefore, it is more appropriate to examine the partial coefficients that control for other independent variables (including urbanization). The partials are not only of the proper sign but are also substantial in size (see Table 7-1). With the ASSBR as dependent, the partial for land availability is second only to urbanization, and for the CBR it is third highest (exceeded by urbanization and e_0). These results are strikingly confirmatory and suggest that this variable, usually excluded from transition theory models, can be quite useful.

With an N of 96 the partial coefficients are all significant at the 1 percent level using the one-tailed t test. With an N of 24 (equal to the number of countries) the significance level drops to 5 percent.

The preferred criterion of examining the unstandardized regression coefficients is difficult to apply, since the measure has no systematic longitudinal association with development or other obvious "normal" range of secular variation. In postwar Latin America the land availability has risen in a few places, fallen slightly in most, and generally not changed very much. The major effect would have to be *across* countries, and a set of hypothetical cross-sectional comparisons will be made.

First, the expected natality differences between pairs of societies with various amounts of land per person were calculated under the assumption that each was 100 percent rural. Results are shown in Table 7-2, which covers the approximate range of land per rural person found in contemporary Latin America. At first

Table 7-2
Natality Differences Implied by Partial Regression on Land Availability

Between Hypothetical Pairs of Countries with Land Per Rural Person of .500 km^2 and:	ASSBR	CBR
.200 km^2	2.45	1.76
.100 km^2	4.30	3.09
.050 km^2	6.16	4.42
.010 km^2	10.46	7.50
.007 km^2	11.41	8.19

glance, the differences in birth rates may seem rather large, but it must be remembered that some of the contrasts in land availability are extreme, and that a completely rural situation is assumed. Comparisons between countries with proportionately equal urban populations and with land per rural person as shown in the table can be made by multiplying the implied natality differences by the proportion urban. Thus, in two countries with 50 percent urban population, implied birth rate differences would be half as great as if each had no urban population. Figures in the table would then be reduced accordingly.

As socioeconomic development occurs, urbanization gradually reduces the numerical significance of the rural sector of the population. The weighting system used takes this process into account by assuming that the influence of the supply of land upon natality decreases with a rise in proportion of the population that is urban. Therefore, it is obvious that urbanization itself affects the measure of land availability and leads to a longitudinal trend associated with socioeconomic development. However, in the present theoretical system it is impossible to discuss the likely impact on natality without also considering the economic expansion variable, since it too is weighted by urbanization (but is assumed to increase in importance with urbanization). The net natality effect of long-term urbanization operating through the weights built into the land availability and economic expansion measures will be discussed at the end of the next section, after the economic expansion variable has been considered separately.

Hypothesis 9: Economic Expansion

Economic expansion (increases in total product weighted by proportion urban) is postulated to have a positive association with natality. Again there was no theoretical reason to expect the relationship to be apparent in the zero-order correlations, but in fact these are both positive and fairly high. The zero-order relationships are contaminated by the correlation with urbanization, however, so that attention should be focused on the partials for which the disturbing influence of urbanization as well as the other variables is controlled.

Table 7-1 shows that the partials are in the expected positive direction. The data suggest that the so-called "business-cycles" effect does have an analog in developing societies. If this is accurate, an upsurge in development could cause a natality increase or delay an impending decline while actually producing the social changes that eventually lead to the demographic transition.

By ordinary significance tests, the partial coefficients reach the .025 level with the ASSBR as dependent and .01 with the CBR if an N of 96 is assumed (one-tailed t test). However, with an N of 24 statistical significance disappears.

The unstandardized regression coefficients indicate a substantial, but believable, impact of economic expansion on natality. If a country were completely urban and the rate of change of the total product moved from stability to an increase of 40 percent per five years, the associated natality increase would be 8.78 for the ASSBR and 6.74 for the CBR. The same economic turnaround in a 70 percent urban country would imply a rise of 6.14 in the ASSBR and 4.72 in the CBR. Such increases may of course delay decreases implied by other variables. Also it should be noted that the model implies that the economic expansion variable, if low in value, can just as easily work the other way, causing premature or temporary natality declines.

Joint Effects of Land Availability and Economic Expansion

The implied natality effects acting through the weights applied to land availability and economic expansion can now be calculated. First we consider the movement of persons from a crowded countryside to urban areas experiencing rapid economic growth—this involves the maximal natality increase.[b] For simplicity we assume that absolute rural population is constant, a situation closely approximated in many Latin American countries. If we then posit land availability of $.10km^2$ per rural person and a 40 percent per five-year rate of GDP growth, an increase from 50 to 70 percent urbanization would suggest a rise of 1.27 in the CBR and 1.74 in the ASSBR. Projected over a probable range of the whole process of urbanization, from 20 to 80 percent urban, the implied natality increase would be 3.82 for the CBR and 5.20 for the ASSBR. These figures are rather modest but not unreasonable given the peripheral nature of the hypothesized effect—the process envisaged is essentially the releasing of constraints that limited birth rates somewhat in a traditional society.

[b]Countries that approximate such conditions include Mexico, where the birth rate does appear to have risen in the postwar era (Collver, 1965), and Costa Rica, where natality seems to have peaked prior to a precipitous decline beginning in the early 1960s (Huyck, 1970).

We encounter an interesting conceptual problem when we consider the implications of the model for a rural population with surplus land undergoing urbanization. The model suggests that this transfer would accelerate the natality decline caused mainly by the modernizing process itself. However, we must determine why a rural populace with plenty of available land should be moving to cities, especially if economic growth should also be slow. The noncomparability of rural and urban life circumstances produces this dilemma. In fact, plentiful land does *not* invariably mean a "good" life to rural people. As development occurs, they presumably acquire new tastes that demand more than land and a secure livelihood. For instance, if persons move from an uncrowded countryside to cities, perhaps in spite of slow economic growth and high unemployment, it may be that they have adopted monetary-materialistic tastes that cannot be satisfied in rural areas. Thus it becomes desirable to exchange even a favorable rural environment for whatever promise the cities hold. The natality effect follows: the agrarian life style could support large families because of plentiful land, but the slow economic growth of the urban areas is not conducive to family life.

Having dealt with the conceptual problems, we proceed to calculate the implied natality impact of urbanization acting as a weighting factor in the case of high land availability and slow economic growth. Again we take absolute rural population to be constant. We posit .500 km^2 land per rural person and slow economic growth of 10 percent in the GDP over five years. The findings then indicate that a 20 percentage point increase in urban population would lower the CBR 1.24 points, and the ASSBR 2.67 points. The cumulative effects over the wider range of urbanization, 20 to 80 percent, would involve a CBR decline of 3.71 and an ASSBR decline of 5.02. Of course these natality decrements are in addition to those brought about by development directly.

The overall implications of the model are more interesting: a country with plentiful land should have high initial natality followed by rapid decline if and when development and urbanization take hold especially if economic conditions are poor during the period. The Soviet Union approximates these characteristics to some extent. In the latter nineteenth century, it was still a frontier nation with vast amounts of land (considerably offset by maldistribution) and slow economic growth. For some time thereafter, urbanization and a poor economic climate coexisted. Although the sparseness of early Russian data precludes a precise test of our prediction, it does appear that natality in Russia fell very quickly from exceedingly high (for Europe) initial levels (Coale, 1969; Kuczynski, 1931).

Problems and Refinements of the Regression Analysis

Linearity

Provided that two variables are monotonically related, as the hypotheses predict, a linear model will seldom produce large distortions in the results even if there are substantial departures from linearity (Labovitz, 1970). Problems will arise only if such departures are systematic and happen to be arrayed in a damaging pattern (i.e., happen to lead to false inferences). Reasonably random errors will tend to underestimate the total predictive power of the model (Blalock, Wells, and Carter, 1970). However, in a multilinear regression, nonlinearity, like measurement error of any sort, can spuriously benefit one independent variable or indicator at the expense of another to the extent that the problem is not equally present in each (Bohrnstedt and Carter, 1971:136-37). To cope with these difficulties, various combinations of monotonic transformations were applied to the independent variables. A set of transformations was sought that came as close as possible to making every relationship linear by seeking the best overall fit. Of those procedures tried, the highest multiple R^2 resulted from raising lagged urbanization, lagged education, lagged expectation of life, and current crude death rate to the 1.5 power while taking the natural logarithms of land availability and economic expansion and leaving lagged product per capita unaltered. This transformed model accounts for 70.4 percent of the variance in the ASSBR, as compared with 65.4 percent obtained with the original variables. For the CBR, explained variance rises to 80.5 percent from 76.7 percent. More detailed results are presented in Table 7-3.

These new findings lead to the same conclusions as the original results in Table 7-1. This suggests that violations of the linearity assumptions, insofar as they follow common functional forms, are not systematically distorting the results, and are only slightly reducing the predictive power of the model. Unfortunately, the apparent predominance of urbanization increases to even higher levels in the transformed system of Table 7-3 as compared with the original variables in Table 7-1. In fact it is generally true that partial correlations that were previously low or moderate in absolute value tend to become slightly smaller under the linearizing transformations, while only the two or three highest partials benefit. Happily, none of the smaller partials becomes so low as to indicate refutation of a hypothesis supported by the original linear model. At this point it seems impossible to determine whether the small differences between Table 7-3 and the original nontransformed results in Table 7-1 are at all meaningful or are simply the result of the peculiarities of measurement errors; but these findings seem to lend more strength to the earlier results.

Lag Times

Since the theory does not specify lag times, an attempt was made to experiment with lags longer than the relatively short 7.5 to 10 years used in the main analysis. However, lengthening the lags (for the lagged variables) does have the undesirable affect of lessening the number of available observations so that results obtained may not be strictly comparable to those produced with shorter lags.

Table 7-3
Results of the Regression Analysis with Variables Monotonically Transformed to Obtain Greater Linearity

| | Dependent Variable | | | |
| | ASSBR | | CBR | |
Independent Variable	Zero-order Correlation	Partial Correlation	Zero-order Correlation	Partial Correlation
Product per capita, lagged 7-1/2 yrs. before natality	−.564[a]	−.025	−.660[a]	−.030
Urbanization, lagged 10 yrs. before natality	−.722[a]	−.566[a]	−.747[a]	−.562[a]
School enrollment, lagged 7-1/2 yrs. before natality	−.454[a]	+.028	−.610[a]	−.075
Crude death rate, contemporaneous with natality	+.462	−.253[a]	+.609	−.236[b]
Expectation of life, lagged 10 yrs. before natality	−.651[a]	−.309[a]	−.793[a]	−.422[a]
Land availability, contemporaneous with natality	+.029	+.423[a]	+.012	+.417[a]
Economic expansion, contemporaneous with natality	+.390[a]	+.204[c]	+.356[a]	+.217[b]

[a]Statistically significant at the .01 level by a one-tailed t test assuming $N = 96$.

[b]Statistically significant at the .025 level by a one-tailed t test assuming $N = 96$.

[c]Statistically significant at the .05 level by a one-tailed t test assuming $N = 96$.

Note: The unstandardized regression coefficients are not shown because they are difficult to interpret or to compare with Table 7-1 after performing the transformations and add no essential information not apparent from the partial correlations. See the text for a listing of the transformations used. See also the note to Table 7-1. Again, the zero-order correlations between the CDR and each dependent variable cannot be significant with a one-tailed t test because of their signs.

Increasing the assumed lag times by five years has relatively little effect on the overall predictive capacity of the model. The variance in natality attributable to the independent variables increases from 65.4 percent to 72.8 percent for the ASSBR and from 76.7 percent to 79.9 percent for the CBR. These increases suggest that longer lags might be more appropriate, but this point remains in doubt due to the smaller sample size available. As sample size decreases, one normally anticipates a slightly better fit. The usual way of dealing with this problem, a correction for degrees of freedom, is inapplicable here, since one must know the true number of independent observations. Since twenty-four cross-sectional units are observed regardless of lag time and the only loss incurred in using longer lags is one time period, it seems unlikely that the number of independent observations lost is very great. Therefore, longer lags do appear to be preferable on the basis of these data, although the improvement is minor.

The particular regression and correlation coefficients remain relatively stable when longer lags are introduced (see Table 7-4). This lends some credence to the predominantly favorable findings produced with shorter lags. Otherwise, there are only three changes of importance.

First, the total explanatory power of the lagged socioeconomic and mortality (e_0) variables rises with the longer lags. This is as expected, since it was presumed that the lag time between changes in these variables and natality were probably longer than originally operationalized. Lags of 12.5 to 15 years do seem to work better than 7.5 to 10 years. If the improvement again seems slight, it should be remembered that the high serial correlation of both independent and dependent variables over short periods means that it is statistically impossible for a five-year alternation in lag time to have a strong impact on the results.

The second major change in Table 7-4 as compared with Table 7-1 lies in the fact that school enrollment has a partial correlation that is in the hypothesized

Table 7-4
Results of the Regression Analysis with Lags Increased by Five Years

| | Dependent Variable | | | |
| | ASSBR | | CBR | |
Independent Variable	Zero-order Correlation	Partial Correlation	Zero-order Correlation	Partial Correlation
Product per capita, lagged 12-1/2 yrs. before natality	−.595[a]	−.042	−.669[a]	−.088
Urbanization, lagged 15 yrs. before natality	−.722[a]	−.592[a]	−.729[a]	−.565[a]
School enrollment, lagged 12-1/2 yrs. before natality	−.511[a]	−.130	−.629[a]	−.226[b]
Crude death rate, contemporaneous with natality	+.510	−.340[a]	+.628	−.291[a]
Expectation of life, lagged 15 yrs. before natality	−.692[a]	−.362[a]	−.795[a]	−.414[a]
Land availability, contemporaneous with natality	−.002	+.392[a]	+.004	+.382[a]
Economic expansion, contemporaneous with natality	+.342[a]	+.137	+.301[a]	+.163

[a]Statistically significant at the .01 level by a one-tailed t test using an assumed N of 72 (the total number of observations for this table).

[b]Statistically significant at the .05 level by a one-tailed t test using an assumed N of 72 (the total number of observations for this table).

Note: Since the purpose of the table is only to provide a comparison with Table 7-1, the raw (unstandardized) regression coefficients would add no information and are not shown. The zero-order correlations for CDR with each dependent variable cannot be significant by a one-tailed t test because of their signs.

direction and of greater magnitude. This means that urbanization no longer completely dominates the three development measures when partial correlations are examined. It seems likely that two factors account for this rather gratifying result. Shrinking the sample size means that the study becomes less longitudinal and more cross-sectional. If, as previously argued, errors caused by conflicting definitions of "urban" are mainly cross-sectional, measurement errors in the urbanization data may become more damaging. On the other hand, it may be the longitudinal irregularities in school enrollment data that are more bothersome. Irregular changes over time may be the result of occasional government drives to increase enrollments, desires to make the data show dramatic improvements, or other discrepancies in school enrollment or the population base by which it is divided to produce the enrollment ratios. In any event, the shift to a more cross-sectional sample allows school enrollment to make a small contribution to explained natality variances even after urbanization is controlled. Although these measurement considerations seem to account for the increased importance of school enrollment and the decreased importance of urbanization with longer lags, it is also possible that a true causal mechanism is involved. Thus, school enrollment may actually take longer to affect natality than urbanization.

Another interesting feature of Table 7-4 is much less easy to explain—the partial correlation of economic expansion and natality decreases. Its sign is still as predicted, but its magnitude (using either natality measure) is small. The only interpretation that seems plausible is based on measurement considerations. Economic expansion is presumably one of the more poorly measured independent variables. Thus as the longer lags improve the predictive capacity of other variables in the system, some variance formerly attributed to economic expansion is lost to the others despite the fact that we have done nothing to the economic expansion measure itself. Considering the crudeness with which the underlying conceptualization has been operationalized, a small coefficient with the hypothesized sign is perhaps all that can be expected.

Even longer lags were tried but the results are not presented in detail since they were similar to those of Table 7-4 except that the trends observed above were slightly stronger. Five more years produced another small increase in total "explained" variance from 72.8 percent to 75.2 percent for the ASSBR and from 79.9 percent to 82.0 percent for the CBR (and again this may be partly or wholly attributable to loss of degrees of freedom). It was again the lagged development and mortality measures that gained the most explanatory power with longer lags. The predominance of urbanization over other aspects of development was further decreased as the partial correlations for both gross domestic product per capita and school enrollment were over −.11 in every case. Finally, the partial correlations of economic expansion and natality dropped below .10 for both natality measures. Reasons for these trends seem to be essentially the same as noted above. Again, lags of 17.5 to 20 years seem better, but now only slightly better, than lags of 12.5 to 15 years, and there is a deleterious effect on the economic expansion variable, presumably due to measurement problems (since this variable is never lagged).

It may well be that the actual causal lags are long, possibly a generation or so. However, the above results tend to substantiate most of the original findings. With the possible exception of economic expansion, the variables seem to operate as predicted regardless of what assumption is made about lag times. Of course it must be remembered that the experimentation with lag times required the exclusion of twenty-four observations for a five-year extension and forty-eight observations for a ten-year extension. Thus, results are not entirely comparable for different lags and the interpretations must be tentative.

Reverse Causation and the
Lagged Variables

Due to the possibility that observed relationships between each of the lagged independent variables and natality could be due to a retarding effect of high natality on development, a new regression that controls for birth rates in the previous five-year period was carried out. This forces the independent variables to explain changes in natality measured by deviations in natality not attributable to past natality. This process controls reverse causation for the lagged but not necessarily the nonlagged independent variables (see Chapter 5). Results appear in Table 7-5.

The signs of all the coefficients are as predicted in hypotheses 5-9. The only change in sign from Table 7-1 is helpful: the positive partial association previously observed between school enrollment and the ASSBR now becomes negative, as predicted by hypothesis 5. The consistency of results obtained with different procedures provides additional support for the theory.

The low coefficients in Table 7-5 are a direct result of the inclusion of past natality as a predictor. Past natality itself "explains" so much of the variance in current natality that the independent variables cannot account for very much. It is necessary to shift perspective when dealing with such an analysis. Instead of attempting to predict the particular values of the dependent variable, the independent variables must account only for deviations not ascribable to the dependent variable in the immediately prior period. This is a much more stringent test of predictive capacity. Thus, the direct effect of past natality "explains" 81.9 percent of the variance in the ASSBR and 81.3 percent in the CBR, leaving only 18.1 percent of the variance in the ASSBR and 18.7 percent in the CBR to work with.[c] Nevertheless, the independent variables still account for 12.0 percent of the variance in the ASSBR and 14.4 percent in the CBR. Two-thirds or more of the variance in the natality deviations are attributable to the independent variables.

[c]The effect of past natality is presumably due to an "inertial" tendency for values to persist.

Table 7-5
Results of the Regression Analysis with Past Natality Controlled

| | Dependent Variable | | | |
| | ASSBR | | CBR | |
Independent Variable	Partial Correlation	Regression Coefficient	Partial Correlation	Regression Coefficient
Product per capita, lagged	−.066	−.002	−.056	−.001
Urbanization, lagged	−.238[a]	−.074[a]	−.215[a]	−.048[a]
School enrollment, lagged	−.095	−.024	−.182[c]	−.034[c]
Crude death rate	−.134	−.163	−.055	−.049
Expectation of life, lagged	−.159	−.119	−.152	−.087
Land availability	+.093	+.293	+.128	+.294
Economic expansion	+.058	+2.302	+.123	+3.627
Natality, lagged	+.905[b]	+.843[b]	+.902[b]	+.819[b]

[a]Statistically significant at the .025 level by a one-tailed t test assuming $N = 94$.

[b]Statistically significant at the .01 level by a one-tailed t test assuming $N = 94$.

[c]Statistically significant at the .05 level by a one-tailed t test assuming $N = 94$.

Note: Since the main purpose of the above table is to show the effects of controlling for past natality, zero-order correlations would not be appropriate. In any event, the zero-order statistics are almost exactly as in Table 7-1, the only differences being very small and the result of excluding two observations in the calculations for Table 7-4. The excluded cases are Haiti and Paraguay 1950-54; no prior natality levels were available for these. See also the note to Table 7-1.

Multicollinearity

Correlations among the independent variables can be found in the Appendix (p. 155). The reader is referred to Chapter 5 for some general remarks; in the present discussion, only the particular intercorrelations we have observed are considered.

The three socioeconomic variables are closely interrelated. This fact has already been considered in attempting to explain urbanization's domination of predictive power. So long as these three variables are considered aspects of a single ongoing phenomenon, multicollinearity presents no difficulties.

Unfortunately, expectation of life at age zero is also highly correlated with the socioeconomic measures and its hypothesized independent effect is important, since infant and child survivorship has a special theoretical position. In defense of the findings, it can be said that the partial coefficients for expectation of life are rather high in absolute value. Therefore, the main effect of multicollinearity, reduction of the reliability of the coefficients, is not likely to be entirely responsible for the confirmation of hypothesis 7. Multicollinearity does pose questions about the true *strength* of the relationship, but the observed coefficients are similar in magnitude regardless of which independent variable or alternative procedure is used. This consistency gives some immunity to the possible damaging effect of lower reliability of the estimators.

The most serious multicollinearity problem stems from the $-.903$ correlation between lagged expectation of life at birth and crude death rate. (Since the CDR is highly correlated with lagged e_0, it is not surprising that it is almost as highly correlated with the lagged development measures. The arguments against the possible distortions of this multicollinearity would be similar to those dealing with the correlation between CDR and e_0.) It is essential that the effects of these variables be separated, since they are hypothesized to be opposite in direction. Again the best defense of the findings would seem to lie in the reasonably large size of the partial coefficients of each of the two variables and the consistency of results with different natality measures, linearizing transformations, various lag times, and control for past natality levels.

Other than those instances discussed above, intercorrelations among the independent variables are not high enough to raise problems. In general, multicollinearity does not cause serious damage to the findings—except possibly for the uncomfortably strong effect ascribed to urbanization by the partials. In this case, the potential for difficulties seems to have been greater than the actuality.

Autocorrelation

Many of the problems that arise when the control for past natality is added (see pp. 138-139) are really due to high probable autocorrelation of the true residuals of natality. Autocorrelation can be corrected if one can guess the approximate pattern of serial dependence on which it is based (see Chapter 5). This means that one must be able to make an assumption about the nature of the variance-covariance matrix of residuals. Following the stated intentions in Chapter 5, an attempt was made to ascertain whether a rather simple set of assumptions was justifiable.

The usual correction for autocorrelation (Wonnacott and Wonnacott, 1970:136-45) assumes that the system of serial dependence is linear and analogous to a first-order Markov chain. This means that each residual is dependent only on the previous residual and is related to still earlier terms only through each immediately prior one. This can be stated more succinctly with an equation. If e stands for the true residual, p for a constant, u for a randomly distributed (nonautocorrelated) error term, and subscripts for time periods, we have:

$$e_t = pe_{t-1} + u_t$$

$$e_{t-1} = pe_{t-2} + u_{t-1}$$

and so forth, or

$$e_t = p^k e_{t-k} + v_t$$

where v_t is a new residual purged of its autocorrelation. Thus, so long as p is within its normal range of 0 to less than 1, the true correlation between any two residuals approaches 0 as the time separating the observations approaches infinity. In the special case $p = 1$, this correlation is constant regardless of time periods.

In order to make the above assumptions, we must first show that the observed autocorrelation across successive pairs of residuals is approximately constant—i.e., that it could have been generated by true residuals in which the autocorrelation across successive pairs is constant. So long as one has only a single unit observed over many periods, common in econometric applications, one cannot make this test directly; however, it is possible to do so with the twenty-four units of the present study. Results are shown in Table 7-6.

Only in the case of the CBR do the correlations appear to be fairly constant. The fact that this does not hold for the ASSBR even though it is supposedly a better measure of natality need not to be too surprising. The ASSBR and CBR could easily have different types of residual components; for instance, the CBR is affected by age structure. Thus, it is quite possible that one would evidence a fairly regular autocorrelation scheme and not the other.

The observed correlations of residuals suggests that P is relatively close to 1 and the values already obtained as the coefficients of lagged natality (.843 and .819 for the ASSBR and CBR respectively) are logical choices as estimates of p—this is known as Durbin's two-stage technique (Durbin, 1960). If the autocorrelation scheme is as hypothesized, therefore, the correlations of natality residuals with lagged natality controlled should be near zero (Johnston, 1973:263). This can be established intuitively by observing that "autocorrelation" means exactly what the term implies: the residual of natality at time t is correlated with the residual of natality at time $t - 1$. To the extent that these residuals are accurately measured, the autocorrelated component of the present residual should be "explained" by the last residual as a predictor of present natality, leaving the resulting residuals free of autocorrelation. (This will be

Table 7-6
Observed Serial Correlations in Residuals

	Age-Sex Standardized Birth Rate			Crude Birth Rate		
Time periods	1, 2	2, 3	3, 4	1, 2	2, 3	3, 4
Correlation	.868	.634	.540	.824	.801	.797

modified to the extent that the measured residuals depart from the true residuals.) This provides a second more stringent and specific test of the first-order Markov assumption. Table 7-7 presents the findings.

The above results are not consistent with the assumption that the true values are uniformly zero, although there is a tendency to approach this ideal for the last two time periods for both natality measures. Further, a comparison with Table 7-6 suggests that for the ASSBR both the apparent magnitude of autocorrelation as well as departure from the first-order Markov assumption may be decreasing over time. This is mildly encouraging, but it does not seem to offer any plausible method for correction of the data. Even under more favorable circumstances, little is known about the estimators that result from data corrected for autocorrelation (Wonnacott and Wonnacott, 1970:143). In view of the fact that the data do not follow any simple or regular autocorrelation system, not much could be gained by applying a correction known to be too simplistic in order to obtain estimators that are dubious even under much better conditions. If the sample consisted of only one time series, this inability to allow for autocorrelation could be very serious. However, the use of twenty-four different units provides a considerable safeguard against the resulting dangers of increased variance of estimators.

Residuals

One final problem became apparent upon examination of the actual values of the residuals in natality (see Appendix). Besides being autocorrelated over time, the magnitude of residuals is higher than a priori expectations. Below are the ten largest residuals from each measure of natality.

Statistically speaking, these errors are not exceptionally large. To calculate the expected number of residuals falling within a given interval, an estimate of the standard error associated with each predicted value is needed. The estimation of standard error requires a knowledge of the true number of independent observations—the true N. Although this is not known, due to autocorrelation, a conservative procedure can be followed by taking the maximal value of $N = 96$,

Table 7-7

Observed Serial Correlations in Residuals after Being Purged of Assumed Linear Autocorrelation from a First-order Markov System

	Age-Sex Standardized Birth Rate			Crude Birth Rate		
Time periods	1, 2	2, 3	3, 4	1, 2	2, 3	3, 4
Correlation	.400	.514	.056	.394	.738	.103

since this minimizes standard error and will make residuals appear larger than if an N below 96 were chosen.[d] This assumption yields a standard error of 5.45 for the estimated ASSBR. This gives a 95 percent confidence interval of plus or minus 10.79 from the predicted ASSBR. We would thus expect about 5 percent of the 96 residuals, or 4.8 of them, to be greater than this amount, and in fact 4 are. Similar calculations for the CBR with its standard error of 3.92 implies that 4.8 residuals should be greater than 7.76 in absolute value, while only 3 are. Therefore the residuals are not distributed so as to produce a statistically abnormal number of extreme values. Rather, what is disturbing is that the residuals indicate a substantial margin of error relative to what would be considered the normal range of natality—this despite what appears to be a "good fit" in terms of R^2.

Two other oddities of the residuals deserve attention: most of the extreme residuals are positive and the aggregate residuals tend to become more positive over time. Thus, 14 of the residuals in Table 7-8 are positive and, on the assumption that each extreme residual had a .5 probability of being of either sign, the probability that 14 or more of the 20 extreme residuals would be of the same sign is only .116. Relative to the second point, the table of residuals (see Appendix) shows that there is a regular pattern of increasing aggregate residuals over the four time periods of observation.

Table 7-8
Extreme Residuals

Age-Sex Standardized Birth Rate		Crude Birth Rate	
Observation	Residual	Observation	Residual
Bolivia 1965-70	−10.21	Brazil 1950-55	−7.62
Colombia 1960-65	+8.98	Colombia 1960-65	+7.05
Costa Rica 1955-60	+11.40	Colombia 1965-70	+7.97
Dominican Rep. 1955-60	+8.79	Costa Rica 1955-60	+6.53
Dominican Rep. 1960-65	+11.63	Costa Rica 1960-65	+7.34
El Salvador 1955-60	+9.52	Jamaica 1950-55	−7.61
Jamaica 1950-1955	−13.46	Mexico 1965-70	+7.29
Mexico 1965-70	+10.13	Uruguay 1950-55	−9.91
Uruguay 1950-55	−12.41	Venezuela 1960-65	+7.34
Venezuela 1965-70	+10.69	Venezuela 1965-70	+9.13

[d]The larger the number of independent observations, the more reliable predicted values should be, because sampling variance is lower in larger samples. By assuming the effective sample size to be the maximum possible value, we minimize assumed sampling variance, and this minimizes the range within which residuals should fall. This makes more residuals statistically "extreme" than would be the case if a smaller sample size were assumed.

These anomalies seem to result from two separate sources. First, the 1950-70 period has not been one of general natality decline in the area. Birth rates fell precipitously in some places but actually rose in others. Meanwhile, socioeconomic development was continuing at a rapid pace almost everywhere. There are three (nontransition theory) variables in the model that are in principle capable of explaining an increase or a delayed decrease in natality (as predicted by lagged development and mortality): short-term mortality changes, land availability, and economic expansion. Of these, land availability is least powerful, because of low longitudinal variance. All three of these variables are more novel than the transition theory variables, and for this reason they may be measured more crudely. Possibly this accounts for an attenuation in their predictive power that causes the natality increases and/or delayed natality declines to go unexplained. Since socioeconomic development and mortality decline are continuing over time, the unexplained aspect of natality becomes more and more positive (natality is underpredicted) until the long-term natality decline finally begins (e.g., Costa Rica).

A second factor involved in the pattern of residuals has already been discussed under hypothesis 4 in the preceding chapter. It seems that there are broad cultural differences that affect natality but are difficult to quantify. Most, but not all, of the effect of culture is mediated by other variables in the model. For reasons discussed in Chapter 6, this cultural factor has not been included in the present regression study. An examination of the natality residuals in light of these cultural differences can be found, however, in Chapter 6, in the discussion of the findings for hypothesis 4.

Conclusions: The Regression
Analysis of Hypotheses 5-9

By the normally accepted statistical standards, even if conservatively interpreted, these hypotheses are strongly supported by the regression analysis. Virtually all of the relationships are consistently in the predicted direction, including some that are seldom if ever dealt with in this type of analysis (hypotheses 6, 8, and 9). Furthermore, the level of predictability is quite high.

Complexities are of course introduced when certain statistical refinements are attempted. These problems should be expected when relatively intricate methodologies are utilized. A great deal of space in this chapter has been given to a consideration of some of these difficulties. This discussion should not obscure the overwhelmingly favorable empirical results.

8

Summary and Conclusions

Previous Theory and Research

This research has attempted to obtain a statement of the theory of the demographic transition that is both theoretical and explicit. Previous investigations have often proceeded without a clear idea of the theory to be tested, and have produced equivocal results for that reason.

The demographic transition is the most important theoretical idea in social demography, yet relatively little effort has been made to organize it into a coherent and testable body of thought. An attempt was made to correct this shortcoming in Chapter 1, in which the existing theoretical ideas were summarized. Only the macroscopic level of analysis was utilized in this effort in the belief that implicit mixing of levels of analysis, the usual practice in transition theory arguments, must ultimately lead to confusion.

Once the theory was stated in a more systematic fashion, it became clear that it cannot explain all the salient features of the European natality experience. The predictions of transition theory are not synonymous with the "European experience," although many investigators use the terms interchangeably. If one were attempting to predict late nineteenth-century European natality on the basis of transition theory, it would be very difficult to predict with much precision either short-term natality fluctuations, which include some fairly large increases, or the time at which a persistent downward trend would become dominant. Furthermore, it would be very hard to make any statement about preexisting natality levels, which vary widely. The evidence presented in Chapter 2 strongly suggests several points. First, it is necessary to use enough indicators of development to get a reasonably broad measure of social change; contradictions implied by one measure may be explained by another. Second, it is necessary to consider mortality as an independent predictor of natality; some problematic events can also be explained by this factor. Third, the notion of lag time must be taken into account. Transition theory includes the supposition that the values governing family size take some time to respond to a new social environment. With this in mind, it is obviously implied that one must examine previous levels of development and mortality to predict natality. These three practices are essential for a faithful application of transition theory as outlined in Chapter 1. The European evidence also suggests that other variables, not part of transition theory, can affect natality. Probably the most obvious example is land availability, which seems to be an important determinant of birth rates, especially in the early development phase. There is also some indication of a business-cycle phenomenon. The very fact that natality can rise before (or after) its major decline demonstrates that forces not a part of the theory are at work. These should be controlled if the theory is to be fairly tested.

When the data pertaining to present-day developing countries were examined in Chapter 3, it became clear that researchers were using very different operationalizations of transition theory. The more obvious and common areas of disagreement involve lag times and the definition of the sample. Conflicting and puzzling results have often arisen from these inconsistencies.

Despite the problems, an examination of past research on developing countries led to several conclusions. First, the development indicators are intended to measure social change. This means that a given variable may not have the same implications for social change everywhere, and results may differ for this reason. This problem is reduced by confining study to cultural regions that are more or less homogeneous. A further benefit of this strategy is the fact that some other sources of measurement error, e.g., differing definitions of "urban," are also less problematic within a single region.

Second, as in Europe, the broadest implications of transition theory do materialize: birth rates are falling in the countries that are relatively developed and have low mortality. However, also as in Europe, natality tends to fluctuate in the predecline period, and sometimes rises substantially, this is especially true in Latin America. It is probable that other variables are responsible for these trends and should be taken into account in the model. When levels of development are controlled, the partial effect of rising national product is to increase natality, an analogue of the business-cycles phenomenon. Short-term economic fluctuations are not equivalent to long-term economic development; their hypothetical natality effects are opposite, and they should be treated separately.

Finally, it has also been demonstrated that the effects of mortality are more complex than first thought. Improving survivorship, especially for adults, and associated improvements in health can raise natality in the short run. Although this effect is widely acknowledged, it is not typically, if ever, included in macroscopic multivariate analyses of natality. The large natality increases that sometimes occur in the early development period may often be attributed, in whole or in part, to the less obvious consequences of mortality decline.

The Revised Causal Model

On the basis of previous theory and research, a new model of natality behavior was formulated in Chapter 4 and means of testing it proposed in Chapter 5. The new theory incorporates many aspects of transition theory, but states these explicitly. Furthermore, these ideas are presented in the form of assumptions that are sufficiently specific to be both meaningful and testable. The basic tenets of transition theory are left intact; it is hypothesized that socioeconomic development and improved survival of infants and children causes, after an intervening lag, a natality decline. In addition, the theoretical model was expanded to deal with the probable effects of land availability, economic expansion rate, and the short-term natality-increasing effect of improved survivorship and health among older persons. Finally, a relevant cultural dimension was identified and summarized as "openness and exposure to modernizing cultural influences." Ultimately, this factor should be broken into various aspects of culture and socioeconomic structure (e.g., family structure and norms about sex roles); however, measurement and statistical problems argued for treating the "culture" variable as a whole.

The model of natality determinants has many possible implications, depending on what additional specific assumptions ("antecedent condition statements") can be made. Some of the basic implications were formulated into nine major hypotheses, which for various reasons were split into two sets.

The first three hypotheses explore the degree to which the occurrence and rate of natality decline can be predicted from levels and rates of change of development and mortality indicators. Since these independent variables are assumed to be the major causes of the long-term natality decline, their effects should be observable without controlling for other variables whose effects are either transitory or cyclic (e.g., economic expansion rate). This is pragmatically important since the data for Latin America before 1950 are too incomplete to allow adequate control of most of these factors. Hypothesis 4 refers to the cultural factor. It, too, is assumed to operate over the long term and to interact with development and mortality to affect natality trends.

Hypotheses 5 through 9 each predict the direction of a given relationship. The basic transition theory variables, in addition to land availability, economic expansion rate, and short-term mortality effects, are taken into account. Largely for statistical and measurement reasons, the cultural index was omitted from this set of hypotheses. With the other independent variables, however, it was possible to execute a longitudinal-cross-sectional regression analysis for all the principal countries of the Latin American region.

Findings

Hypotheses 1-3, tested in Chapter 6, represent only a slight departure from some of the older versions of demographic transition theory. This study has applied these ideas to an area of the developing world where there were many indications that they would not prove very predictive of natality trends. Although there are limits to the theory's power, the findings suggest that transition theory works quite well in modern Latin America.

Specific Hypotheses

The rates of natality decline in Latin America as a whole, especially after 1950, are in line with predictions, but comparisons among Latin American countries present difficulties. Natality declines in Latin America have been more rapid than in northwestern Europe or Italy and much more rapid than in the Iberian nations, thus confirming hypotheses 1a-1c; however, this finding holds much more strongly for post-World-War-II Latin America, and it was suggested in Chapter 6 that these hypotheses would have essentially the same causal implications if confined to this period. Rates of natality decline in the various countries of Latin America are somewhat related to rates of change of development measures, mildly supporting hypothesis 2b, but not at all related to mortality decline rates as measured, thus refuting hypothesis 2a.

The problems experienced with hypotheses 2a and 2b led to the identification of a very important trend in the Latin American data: both the rate of increase in development and the rate of decrease in mortality have accelerated over time. In the most recent periods, rates of change are unprecedented by historical standards. This acceleration has been very rapid for mortality, and may well explain the failure of hypothesis 2a. Mortality decline rates are quite similar across countries with similar absolute levels at any given time, and current rates of decline are just about as rapid as can be obtained with present technology. In general, rates of change of development and mortality do not predict cross-country differences in the pace of natality decline. However, it may be more significant that the accelerating rates of development and mortality reduction have been followed by accelerating and extremely rapid rates of natality decline in those countries where natality decline has begun. Interestingly enough, this acceleration is not a new phenomenon, but an extension and amplification of trends of social and demographic change that were first noticed in comparing northwestern, central, and eastern Europe (Chapter 2). In Latin America, this acceleration has become so pronounced that it tends to obscure all other aspects of the data; nevertheless, the relationships posited by transition theory could have produced the natality trends observed.

Relative levels of development and mortality predict quite dependably the identity of those countries most likely to begin natality decline; hypothesis 3 is supported. Nevertheless, there were some countries in which natality decline had not clearly begun but which appeared to be "ready" in terms of development and mortality (or fast becoming so), even allowing for lag time. It is gratifying that since the time when these calculations were first made, examination of 1970 census materials has discovered evidence of natality decline in both Brazil and Venezuela, in accordance with prior predictions. As yet no comparable decline is apparent in Mexico, for which the same prediction had been made, but the trend of falling birth rates now appears to be spreading to some of the larger nations of mainland Latin America.

The openness and exposure of cultures to modernizing influences, as indexed by racial composition, strongly affects the timing of socioeconomic development, mortality decline, and natality decline. Latin American countries populated mainly by Europeans were the first to experience development and mortality decline, and all have reduced birth rates as well. Several African-East Indian countries of the region have tended to experience fairly early development and mortality decline, and most have begun to reduce natality (since World War II). The mestizo, and even more the Amerindian societies, were generally the last to undergo significant socioeconomic development and mortality decline. Natality reduction is a very recent phenomenon, to the extent that it has even appeared, among countries of these cultural groups. Generally speaking, the effect of cultural background operates through socioeconomic development and mortality; however, there is some direct effect as well. Controlling for development and mortality, the European and African-East Indian countries tend to have low natality (that is, they have lower natality than predicted by the other variables in the causal system); mestizo countries have high natality; and Amerindian countries have moderate natality.

Cultural background as measured by racial composition encompasses many dimensions that might account for the effects we have observed; however, the most obvious, religion, does not seem crucial. The European and mestizo countries share the Catholic religion, but behave much differently. Further, it is the European group that seems most influenced by Catholicism, and yet these nations were the first to reduce natality. The African-East Indian countries, where the Catholic Church is the weakest, display characteristics that place them somewhere between the Catholic Europeans and Catholic mestizos. No systematic association between religion and natality can be seen.

Differences in family structure and sex roles seem more likely explanations for the direct effect of culture on natality. The combination of the chauvanist values, greatly different standards of sexual conduct for men and women, and the disruption of the indigenous social structure seems to have led to high natality, high illegitimacy, and very high birth rates at young ages in the mestizo nations. It is expected that these countries should maintain very high natality up to the beginning of natality decline, with rapid reductions thereafter. (Costa Rica, which would be considered mestizo except for a rather large number of Europeans, displays this trend and perhaps belongs in this group.) The Amerindian countries may follow this trend also, but some years later; in the meantime their natality levels may rise.

The findings of Chapter 6 convey the impression that the basic causal forces posited are operating as expected. Historical factors have introduced a new dimension, however, in that the whole process of change has accelerated. The cultural backgrounds of various countries also create a complication, but this factor seems to become less important as development progresses. There is every indication that the fundamental causal relationships that presumably brought about the European natality decline have been at work in the Latin American region.

Recent Natality Trends and
Simultaneous Operationalization
of Independent Variables

The present research includes a pooled cross-sectional and longitudinal multivariate analysis. This was used to operationalize hypotheses 5-9 simultaneously in an attempt to explain the post-World-War-II natality behavior of the major countries of the Latin American region.

This procedure was successful in that about 75 percent of the variance in natality can be attributed to the seven independent variables, and all the individual relationships are in the predicted direction. Lagged socioeconomic development and long-term improvements in survivorship (measured by e_0) do tend to reduce natality substantially. Urbanization has more explanatory power than the other two development measures (GDP per capita and school enrollment); however, this can probably be attributed to measurement rather than causal considerations. The errors in measuring "percentage urban" become less crucial when several observations are made on the same country, as in this research, while longitudinal changes in gross domestic product per capita and school enrollment are more irregular. When longer lags are introduced, thus reducing the number of sequential observations and making the analysis more cross-sectional, the special importance of urbanization is mitigated.

This research also introduced three independent variables known to affect natality but not usually included in models based on transition theory. Measures had to be devised for these variables. As predicted, it was found that the greater the availability of land and the rate of economic expansion, the higher the natality, controlling for the other variables in the model. It was also found that short-term changes in mortality tend to raise natality initially. As anticipated, none of these three effects is as important as the combined effect of development or long-term mortality decline, but all three relationships are reasonably strong by the usual statistical standards.

The present regression model also allowed the calculation of cross-lag coefficients, which represent the effect of the independent variables upon natality when previous natality is controlled. This helps to control for possible distortions introduced by reverse causation and certain types of autocorrelation. This technique is relatively new in social research, however, and new interpretations must be attached to the cross-lag coefficients, which are almost always small in size. Nevertheless, the independent variables of the model do predict most of the variance in natality *not* accounted for by past natality—i.e, the deviations are very predictable. Furthermore, there is no evidence that reverse causation has created spurious inference.

The present model also allowed some experimentation with lag times and forms of causal relationships. The full potential of these advantages was not realized in this study, presumably because the time period observed was too short and the relationships were largely linear. The length of lag has relatively little impact since natality and the lagged independent variables are highly correlated with their own values over time. Thus it makes little statistical difference whether a lag of ten years or fifteen years is used except that, in the present case, some observations are lost due to the limited availability of data. Similarly, little change results from substituting different forms of relationships. For the period since World War II, linear associations work almost as well as any of those tried.

General Implications

The theory of the demographic transition has received strong empirical support in the present study. However, no theory can encompass all phenomena within its scope, and in particular no social theory is likely to explain all the salient features of a particular phenomenon. If other variables known to affect the birth rate but not a part of older versions of transition theory are also included in a model, predictability can be enhanced. In attempting to systematically present and improve upon the transition theory model of natality behavior, this investigation has sought to correct a deficiency that plagues much sociodemographic research in this field.

It is also suggested that social demographers could make greater use of more sophisticated statistical techniques adapted from econometrics. The mathematical structure of macroscopic econometric models does not differ fundamentally from that suggested by theories of natality behavior articulated at the societal level. While formal demographers have made use of sophisticated methods and mathematical models, social demography has been noticeably lacking in this area. This research has sought to make a contribution by employing a pooled cross-sectional-longitudinal multivariate analysis which allows a more valid operationalization and more exacting test of the underlying theoretical model than strictly cross-sectional techniques.

To me the most important contribution of this analysis lies in demonstrating the power of theory, even rather primitive theory, when explicitly applied to an appropriate data base. The preponderance of results in this research support transition theory predictions and lead to the expectation of widespread and precipitous natality decline in the Latin American region. The conflicting, often puzzling findings of many past investigations can, I believe, be traced to inadequate theoretical development. If we rely on blind empiricism, we relegate ourselves to description, and rather slow description at that, in view of the time necessary to collect and refine demographic data. Sometimes even a crude prediction can be infinitely more valuable than the most sophisticated projection, since the former is guided by theory and empirical research. If we do not seek explanations we are doomed to follow in the wake of events rather than toward control of our environment. In this sense the theoretical is perfectly compatible with the practical.

Even the most rapid natality decline imaginable will not end the problem of excessive population growth in Latin America for some time to come, because of the tremendous growth in the size of young cohorts already built into the age structure. The present results should in no way be interpreted as a recommendation to reduce effort toward providing adequate contraceptive technology to all who wish it. On the contrary, Latin American nations cannot afford to follow the slower pattern of European natality decline, because the pace of mortality reduction has been so greatly accelerated. And while the concomitantly rapid and accelerating rate of socioeconomic change holds promise, it also harbors dangers, not the least of which are chaos on the one hand and repression on the other. Far from being stagnant, Latin America is experiencing massive change in social and economic terms as well as demographic; it is worthy of more systematic study.

Appendix

Appendix

Table A-1
Matrix of Zero-order Correlations

	GDP	% Urban	Education	CDR	e_0	Land	Expansion
% Urban	.608						
Education	.639	.432					
CDR	−.702	−.594	−.743				
e_0	.734	.641	.819	−.903			
Land	−.014	−.341	−.072	.043	.002		
Expansion	−.075	.281	.004	−.018	−.124	−.224	
ASSBR	−.564	−.687	−.451	.492	−.633	.022	.346
CBR	−.660	−.720	−.611	.641	−.778	.027	.310

Note: GDP, % Urban, and Education are lagged seven and one-half years; e_0 is lagged ten years; other variables are contemporaneous with the birth rate.

GDP = gross domestic product per capita in 1963 U.S. dollars.

% Urban = percentage of the population said to be "urban".

CDR = deaths per year per 1000 population.

e_0 = expectation of life at birth for both sexes.

Land = the natural logarithm of the total land per 1000 rural persons multiplied by the proportion of the population said to be "rural".

Expansion = the ratio of absolute national product at a given time and its value five years previously multiplied by the proportion of the population said to be "urban".

ASSBR = age-sex standardized birth rate—see United Nations (1956:42-44).

CBR = births per year per 1000 population.

Table A-2
Residuals (Deviations) of the ASSBR Regressed on the Independent Variables

Period	Argentina	Bolivia	Brazil	Chile	Colombia	Costa Rica
			Country			
1950-54	−8.05	−5.87	−7.70	+1.63	+2.35	+5.74
1955-59	−.96	−3.96	−3.71	+2.66	+8.57	+11.40
1960-64	−2.96	−2.98	+.30	−.51	+8.98	+2.06
1965-69	−6.92	−10.21	−3.14	−.95	+.81	−5.35

	Cuba	Dominican Republic	Ecuador	El Salvador	Guatemala	Guyana
1950-54	−8.04	+1.82	+4.02	+3.43	+.66	−1.31
1955-59	−3.32	+8.79	+4.67	+9.52	+1.89	−2.55
1960-64	−5.20	+11.63	+5.11	+7.30	+5.34	−5.48
1965-69	−.76	−.46	+.78	+.17	−5.30	−6.09

	Haiti	Honduras	Jamaica	Mexico	Nicaragua	Panama
1950-54	−6.87	+1.59	−13.46	+.93	−2.84	−2.65
1955-59	−2.91	+1.55	−6.81	+1.00	−.29	−.62
1960-64	−1.13	+2.14	+3.12	+6.97	−.47	+3.34
1965-69	−2.49	+3.74	+4.71	+10.13	+3.06	+3.20

	Paraguay	Peru	Puerto Rico	Trinidad & Tobago	Uruguay	Venezuela
1950-54	+2.57	+.85	−4.53	−4.47	−12.41	−6.93
1955-59	+5.77	−.11	−1.66	−4.08	−6.86	−1.25
1960-64	+5.50	+1.96	−3.37	−2.98	−.81	+8.53
1965-69	+4.52	+2.43	−4.08	−2.93	+2.87	+10.69

Note: Each figure is the difference between a predicted and an actual value of the ASSBR (age-sex standardized birth rate). The independent variables are as listed in the note to Table A-1.

Table A-3
Residuals (Deviations) of the CBR Regressed on the Independent Variables

			Country			
Period	Argentina	Bolivia	Brazil	Chile	Colombia	Costa Rica
1950-54	−4.37	−3.78	−7.62	−.19	+1.29	+2.62
1955-59	−6.11	−3.83	−5.89	+2.34	+4.27	+6.53
1960-64	−1.24	−2.69	−2.96	+2.44	+7.05	+7.34
1965-69	−3.39	−2.47	+.19	−.79	+7.97	+.14
	Cuba	Dominican Republic	Ecuador	El Salvador	Guatemala	Guyana
1950-54	−3.26	+.33	+.76	+3.31	−.34	−3.33
1955-59	−5.95	+2.44	+3.13	+5.30	−1.32	−1.11
1960-64	−2.46	+6.22	+2.60	+5.78	−1.44	−2.16
1965-69	−3.39	+8.30	+2.27	+2.81	+1.09	−3.41
	Haiti	Honduras	Jamaica	Mexico	Nicaragua	Panama
1950-54	−3.78	+.44	−7.61	+2.57	−.27	−.84
1955-59	−3.08	−.28	−2.75	+1.57	−2.08	+.01
1960-64	−1.69	−.34	+1.91	+4.83	−2.34	+.78
1965-69	−1.37	+1.19	+.76	+7.29	−.06	+.74
	Paraguay	Peru	Puerto Rico	Trinidad & Tobago	Uruguay	Venezuela
1950-54	+3.07	−.19	−3.82	−1.95	−9.91	−4.89
1955-59	+3.48	−.47	−2.14	−2.53	−5.13	−.98
1960-64	+3.23	−.28	−1.73	−1.58	−1.00	+7.34
1965-69	+3.61	+.74	−1.92	−2.03	+1.30	+9.13

Note: Each figure is the difference between a predicted and an actual value of the CBR (crude birth rate). The independent variables are as listed in the note to Table A-1.

Table A-4
Natality Declines in Latin America as Measured by the Crude Birth Rate

| Period | Early Natality Declines Crude Birth Rate | | | |
	Argentina	Chile	Cuba	Uruguay
1875-79	45.6			
1880-84	45.0	48.0		
1885-89	44.6	46.6		
1890-94	42.9	45.9		
1895-99	42.4	45.0		43.4
1900-1904	41.0	44.7		38.9
1905-1909	40.0	44.6	47.4	37.6
1910-1914	40.3	44.4	44.7	36.5
1915-1919	36.1	43.3	40.7	31.9
1920-1924	34.3	42.2	36.7	30.1
1925-1929	32.4	43.8	32.9	28.6
1930-1934	28.9	40.2	31.3	25.8
1935-1939	25.7	38.4	30.9	22.3
1940-1944	25.7	38.3	31.9	21.6
1945-1949	25.2	37.0	30.0	21.1
1950-1954	25.4	38.8	31.5	22.0
1955-1959	24.1	37.8	30.0	22.4
1960-1964	22.5	35.9	28.1	22.1
1965-1969	21.0	30.6	26.6	21.3

Table A-4 (cont.)

Possible Natality Declines
(countries with annual data)

Crude Birth Rate

Year	El Salvador	Guatemala	Guyana	Panama
1951		50.9		
1952		52.3		
1953		50.9	44.1	
1954		51.3	42.9	
1955		48.6	43.2	
1956		48.4	43.1	
1957	50.9	49.0	43.8	
1958	49.6	48.2	43.8	
1959	48.5	49.2	43.7	
1960	49.5	48.9	42.2	
1961	49.4	49.3	42.1	40.4
1962	48.4	47.3	42.7	41.1
1963	49.0	47.3	42.0	40.5
1964	47.1	45.6	40.3	39.9
1965	46.9	45.3	39.7	39.4
1966	45.4	45.4	39.8	38.4
1967	44.4	42.8	36.5	38.2
1968	43.2	43.5	36.3	38.3
1969	42.1	43.0		37.9
1970	39.8	39.0		37.1
1971	43.5	41.7		37.2
1972	40.7			35.6

Estimated Brazilian Birth Rates

Period	Crude Birth Rate (U.N.)	Crude Birth Rate (Oechsli)
1950-55	42.2	41.2
1955-60	40.3	40.3
1960-65	38.5	39.8
1965-70	37.8	37.4

Estimated Venezuelan Birth Rates

Period	Crude Birth Rate (U.N.)	Period	Crude Birth Rate (Oechsli)
1950-55	42.7	1952-56	45.1
1955-60	42.5	1957-61	46.3
1960-65	41.8	1962-66	43.6
1965-70	40.9	1967-71	39.9

Note: Data sources are as described in the notes to Table 6-3, the "Oechsli" series for Brazil is from Oechsli and Adlahka, 1974, and for Venezuela, from Oechsli and Edmonston, 1974.

Table A-4 (cont.)

Recent Natality Declines

(countries with annual data)

Crude Birth Rate

Year	Chile	Costa Rica	Jamaica	Puerto Rico	Trinidad and Tobago
1949				42.1	
1950				41.7	
1951				40.3	
1952				38.5	
1953				37.6	
1954				37.3	41.9
1955		48.9		36.5	41.9
1956		48.5		36.6	37.0
1957	36.8	47.9		35.3	37.7
1958	36.0	47.2		33.6	37.6
1959	35.8	48.3	39.9	33.6	37.4
1960	35.7	47.4	42.0	33.5	39.5
1961	35.9	47.9	40.2	32.3	37.9
1962	35.7	46.6	39.1	32.0	37.9
1963	35.2	45.9	39.0	31.5	35.6
1964	34.1	43.0	39.2	31.2	34.7
1965	33.2	42.3	38.9	30.7	32.8
1966	31.6	40.9	38.8	28.0	30.2
1967	30.9	39.0	35.9	26.5	28.2
1968	26.6	36.2	34.3	25.3	27.5
1969	N.A.	34.4	33.1	24.9	24.5
1970	29.6	33.2	34.4	24.8	24.5
1971		31.6	34.8	25.6	23.9
1972		31.6	34.6	24.1	25.1
Base[a]	36.2[b]	48.9	40.9	42.5	40.5

[a]The base is the maximum post-1947 three-year moving average; for each country this period has as its middle year the first year for which a datum appears above.

[b]For Chile the true "base" is the prewar five-year estimated maximum which was 48.0 in 1880-84; the figure shown here would apply if the prewar decline were ignored.

Bibliography

Bibliography

Abhayaratne, O.E.R., and C.H.S. Jayewardene. *Fertility Trends in Ceylon.* Colombo: Colombo Apothecaries Co., 1968.

Adelman, Irma. "An Econometric Analysis of Population Growth." *American Economic Review*, 53:314-39, 1963.

_____, and Cynthia Morris. "A Quantitative Study of Social and Political Determinants of Fertility." *Economic Development and Cultural Change*, 14:129-57, 1966.

Alker, Hayward R., Jr. "A Typology of Ecological Fallacies." *Quantitative Ecological Analysis in the Social Sciences*. Edited by M. Dogan and S. Rokan. Cambridge: M.I.T. Press, 1969.

Arriaga, Eduardo E. *New Life Tables for Latin American Populations in the Nineteenth and Twentieth Centuries*. Berkeley: Institute of International Studies, University of California, Population Monograph Series Number 3, 1968.

_____. *Mortality Decline and Its Demographic Effects in Latin America.* Berkeley: Institute of International Studies, University of California, Population Monograph Series Number 6, 1970a.

_____. "The Nature and Effects of Latin America's Non-Western Trend in Fertility." *Demography*, 7:483-501, 1970b.

Banks, Arthur S. *Cross-Polity Time Series Data.* Cambridge: M.I.T. Press, 1971.

Basavarajappa, K.G. "The Influence of Fluctuations in Economic Conditions on Fertility and Marriage Rates, Australia, 1920-21 to 1937-38 and 1946-47 to 1966-67." *Population Studies*, 25:39-53, 1971.

Beshers, J.M. *Population Processes in Social Systems.* New York: Free Press, 1967.

Blake, Judith. "Demographic Science and the Redirection of Public Policy." *Journal of Chronic Diseases*, 18:1181-1200, 1965.

Blalock, H.M., Caryll S. Wells, and Lewis F. Carter. "Statistical Estimation with Random Measurement Error." In *Sociological Methodology, 1970*, edited by Edgar F. Borgatta and George W. Bohrnstedt, pp. 75-103. San Francisco: Jossey-Bass, 1970.

Bogue, Donald. "The End of the Population Explosion." *The Public Interest*, 7:11-20, 1967.

Bohrnstedt, George W. "Observations on the Measurement of Change." In *Sociological Methodology, 1969*, edited by Edgar F. Borgatta, pp. 113-33. San Francisco: Jossey-Bass, 1969.

Caldwell, John C. "Fertility Attitudes in Three Contrasting Rural Regions of Ghana." *Economic Development and Cultural Change*, 15:224-32, 1967.

_____. "The Control of Family Size in Tropical Africa." *Demography*, 5:598-619, 1968.

Carlsson, Gösta. "Decline of Fertility: Innovation or Adjustment Process." *Population Studies*, 20:149-74, 1966.

Carr-Saunders, A.M. *World Population: Past Growth and Present Trends.* Oxford: Clarendon Press, 1936.

CELADE (Centro Latinoamericano de Demografía). *Boletín Demográfico Año. 1*, Vol. 2, 1968.

Clark, Colin. *The Conditions of Economic Progress.* 3rd ed. London: Macmillan Co., 1957.

Clifford, William B., II. "Modern and Traditional Value Orientations and Fertility Behavior: A Social Demographic Study." *Demography*, 8:37-48, 1971.

Coale, Ansley J. "The Decline of Fertility in Europe from the French Revolution to World War II." Pp. 3-24 in *Fertility and Family Planning: A World Review.* Edited by S.J. Behrman, L. Corsa, Jr., and R. Freedman. Ann Arbor: University of Michigan Press, 1969.

_____, and E.M. Hoover. *Population Growth and Development in Low Income Countries.* Princeton: Princeton University Press, 1958.

Collver, O. Andrew. *Birth Rates in Latin America: New Estimates of Historical Fluctuations.* Berkeley: Institute of International Studies, University of California, Research Series Number 7, 1965.

Cowgill, Donald O. "Transition Theory as General Population Theory." *Social Forces*, 41:270-74, 1963.

Davis, Kingsley. "Population." *Scientific American*, 209:62-71, 1963.

_____. *World Urbanization 1950-1970.* Vol. I. *Basic Data for Cities, Countries, and Regions.* Berkeley: Institute of International Studies, University of California, Population Monograph Series Number 4, 1969.

_____, and Judith Blake. "Social Structure and Fertility: An Analytical Framework." *Economic Development and Cultural Change*, 4:211-35, 1956.

Demeny, Paul. "Early Fertility Decline in Austria-Hungary: A Lesson in Demographic Transition." *Daedalus*, 97:502-22, 1968.

Durbin, J. "Estimation of Parameters in Time-series Regression Models." *Journal of the Royal Statistical Society, Series B*, 22:139-53, 1960.

Easterlin, Richard A. "The American Baby Boom in Historical Perspective." *American Economic Review*, 51:869-911, 1961.

_____. "On the Relation of Economic Factors to Recent and Projected Fertility." *Demography*, 3:131-53, 1969.

_____. "Does Population Adjust to Environment?" *American Economic Review*, 61:399-407, 1971.

Fairchild, Henry P. *People.* New York: Holt and Company, 1939.

Fleiger, Wilhelm. "A Re-Examination of the Demographic Transition in the Light of Newly Collected Data." Unpublished doctoral dissertation, University of Chicago, December 1967.

Forni, Floreal H. "Review of J.M. Stycos, *Human Fertility in Latin America:*

Sociological Perspectives." Economic Development and Cultural Change,
19:128-35, 1970.

Freedman, Ronald. "The Sociology of Human Fertility: A Trend Report and a
Bibliography." *Current Sociology*, 10-11, 1961-62.

_____. "Norms for Family Size in Underdeveloped Areas." *Proceedings of
the Royal Society*, 159:220-34, 1963.

Friedlander, Dov. "Demographic Responses and Population Change." *Demography*, 6:359-81, 1969.

Friedlander, Stanley, and Morris Silver. "A Quantitative Study of the Determinants of Fertility Behavior." *Demography*, 4:30-70, 1970.

Galbraith, V.L., and D.S. Thomas. "Birth Rates and the Interwar Business
Cycles." *Journal of the American Statistical Association*, 36:465, 1941.

Galton, Francis. "Commenting on Edward B. Tylor, 'On a Method of Investi-
gating the Development of Institutions Applied to the Laws of Marriage and
Descent." *Journal of the Royal Anthropological Institute*, 18:272, 1889.

Goldscheider, Calvin. *Population, Modernization, and Social Structure.* Boston:
Little, Brown and Company, 1971.

Goode, William. "Illegitimacy, Anomie, and Cultural Penetration." *American
Sociological Review*, 26:910-25, 1961.

_____. *The Family.* Englewood Cliffs, N.J.: Prentice-Hall, Inc., 1964.

Goubert, Pierre. "Legitimate Fecundity and Infant Mortality in France during
the Eighteenth Century: A Comparison." *Daedalus*, 97:593-603, 1968.

Habakkuk, H.J. "English Population in the Eighteenth Century." *Economic
History Review*, 6:117-33, 1958.

Hajnal, J. "European Marriage Patterns in Perspective." in *Population in History*,
edited by D.V. Glass and D.E.C. Eversley. Chicago: Aldine Publishing Co.,
1965.

Hanley, Susan B. "Population Trends in Tokugawa Japan: The Base of Bizen
Province in Okayama." *Daedalus*, 97:622-35, 1968.

Hannan, Michael. "Problems of Aggregation." Pp. 473-508 in *Causal Models in
the Social Sciences*. Edited by H.M. Blalock. Chicago: Alpine-Atherton, 1971.

Hauser, Philip M. "Urbanization—Problems of High Density Living." *World
Population—The View Ahead.* Edited by R.N. Farmer, J.D. Long, and G.J.
Stolnitz. Bloomington: Bureau of Business Research, Indiana University,
1968.

Hawthorne, Geoffrey. *The Sociology of Fertility.* London: Collier-Macmillan,
1970.

Heer, David M. "Fertility Differences between Indian and Spanish-Speaking
Parts of Andean Countries." *Population Studies*, 18:71-84, 1964.

Heer, David M. "Economic Development and Fertility." *Demography*, 3:423-44,
1966.

_____, and E.S. Turner. "Areal Differences in Latin American Fertility."
Population Studies, 18:279-92, 1965.

Heise, David R. "Causal Inference from Panel Data." Pp. 3-27 in *Sociological Methodology, 1970*. Edited by Edgar F. Borgatta and George W. Bohrnstedt. San Francisco: Jossey-Bass, 1970.

Helleiner, K.F. "The Vital Revolution Reconsidered." *Population in History*. Edited by D.V. Glass and D.E.C. Eversley. Chicago: Aldine Publishing Co., 1965.

Hexter, M.B. *Social Consequences of Business Cycles*. New York: Houghton Mifflin, 1925.

Himes, Norman E. *Medical History of Contraception*. New York: Schocken Books, 1963.

Hofstee, E.W. "Regionale Vercheidenheid in de Ontwikkeling van het Aantal Gerboorten in Nederland in de 2e Helft van de 19e Eeuw." *Koninklijke Nederland Akademie van Wetenschappen, Akademiedagen*, 7, 1954.

Homans, George C. *English Villagers of the Thirteenth Century*. Cambridge, Mass.: Harvard University Press, 1941.

Huyck, Earl E. "Fertility and Family Planning: The Costa Rica Case." Paper presented at the annual meeting of the Population Association of America, Atlanta, Georgia, April 17, 1970.

Hyrenius, D.H. "The Relation between Birth Rates and Economic Activity in Sweden, 1920-1944." *Bulletin of the Oxford University Institute of Statistics*, 8:14-21, 1946.

International Bank for Reconstruction and Development. *Trends in Developing Countries*. Washington, D.C.: International Bank, 1970.

Ipola, S. Torrado de. "Natalidad y Fecundidad en Argentina desdefines del siglo XIX." Paper presented at the Conferenciá Regional Latino Americana de Población, 1970.

Jain, A.K., T.C. Hsu, R. Freedman, and M.C. Chang. "Demographic Aspects of Lactation and Postpartum Amenorrhea." *Demography*, 7:255-71, 1970.

James, Preston E. *Latin America*. 4th ed. New York: Odyssey Press, 1969.

Janowitz, Barbara S. "An Empirical Study of the Effects of Socioeconomic Development on Fertility Rates." *Demography*, 8:319-34, 1971.

Johnston, J. *Econometric Methods*. 2nd ed. New York: McGraw-Hill, 1972.

Kirk, Dudley. *Europe's Population in the Interwar Years*. Princeton: League of Nations, 1946.

_____. "The Influence of Business Cycles on Marriage and Birth Rates." *Demographic and Economic Change in Developed Countries*. National Bureau of Economic Research. Princeton: Princeton University Press, 1960.

_____. "Factors Affecting Moslem Natality." Pp. 561-79 in *Family Planning and Population Programs*. Edited by Bernard Berelson, et al. Chicago: University of Chicago Press, 1966.

_____. "A New Demographic Transition?" In *Rapid Population Growth— Consequences and Public Policy Implications*. National Academy of Sciences, pp. 123-47. Baltimore: Johns Hopkins University Press, 1971.

_____, and S. Beaver. "The Accelerating Decline of Natality in the Demographic Transition." Unpublished paper, Food Research Institute, Stanford University, California, 1971.

_____, and D.L. Nortman. "Business and Babies: The Influence of the Business Cycle on Birth Rates." *Proceedings of the American Statistical Association, Social Statistics Section*, pp. 151-60, 1958.

_____, and K.S. Srikantan. "Correlates of Natality in Countries of the Latin American Region." Unpublished paper, Food Research Institute, Stanford University, California, 1969.

Kiser, Clyde V., W.H. Grabill, and A.A. Campbell. *Trends and Variations in Fertility in the United States.* Cambridge, Mass.: Harvard University Press, 1968.

Krause, J.T. "Some Implications of Recent Work in Historical Demography." *Comparative Studies in Society and History*, 1:164-88, 1957.

Kuczynski, Robert R. *The Balance of Births and Deaths.* Vols. I and II. Washington: The Brookings Institution, 1928 and 1931.

_____. *The Measurement of Population Growth.* New York: Oxford University Press, 1936.

Kuhn, Thomas S. *The Structure of Scientific Revolution.* Chicago: University of Chicago Press, 1962.

Kuznets, Simon. *Postwar Economic Growth.* Cambridge, Mass.: Harvard University Press, 1964.

Labovitz, Sanford. "The Assignment of Numbers to Rank Order Categories." *American Sociological Review*, 35:515-24, 1970.

Leasure, J.W. "Factors Involved in the Decline of Fertility in Spain 1900-1950." *Population Studies*, 16:271-85, 1963.

Livi Bacci, Massimo. "Contribution à l'étude des Facteurs Sociaux de la Fécondité Européenne." *Genus*, 22:225-55, 1966.

_____. "Fertility and Nuptiality Changes in Spain from the Late 18th to the Early 20th Century, Part I." *Population Studies*, 22:83-102, 1968a.

_____. "Fertility and Nuptiality Changes in Spain from the Late 18th to the Early 20th Century, Part II." *Population Studies*, 22:211-34, 1968b.

_____. "Fertility and Population Growth in Spain in the Eighteenth and Nineteenth Centuries." *Daedalus*, 97:523-35, 1968c.

_____. *A Century of Portuguese Fertility.* Princeton: Princeton University Press, 1971.

Lorimer, Frank, et al. *Culture and Human Fertility.* Zurich: UNESCO, 1954.

McGranahan, D.V. "Analysis of Socioeconomic Development through a System of Indicators." *The Annals of the American Academy of Political and Social Sciences*, 393:65-81, 1971.

Mackenroth, Gerhard. *Bevölkerungslehre: Theorie, Soziologie und Statistik der Bevolkerung.* Berlin: Springer Verlag, 1953.

Malthus, T.R. *An Essay on the Principle of Population.* 1st ed., 1798.

Malthus, T.R. *An Essay on the Principle of Population.* 2nd ed., 1803.

_____. *Principles of Political Economy Considered with View to Their Practical Application.* 2nd ed., 1836.

Merton, Robert K. *Social Theory and Social Structure.* Rev. ed. Glencoe: The Free Press, 1957.

Mill, John S. *Principles of Political Economy.* Vol. I, 1864.

Morgenstern, Oskar. *On the Accuracy of Economic Observations.* 2nd ed. Princeton: Princeton University Press, 1963.

Murumatsu, Minoru. *Japan's Experience in Family Planning—Past and Present.* Tokyo: Family Planning Federation of Japan, 1967.

Naroll, Raoul. "Two Solutions to Galton's Problem." *Philosophy of Science,* 28:15-39, 1961.

_____. "Some Thoughts on Comparative Cultural Anthropology." In *Methodology in Social Research,* edited by H.M. and A.B. Blalock, pp. 236-77. New York: McGraw-Hill Book Company, Inc., 1968.

National Academy of Science. *The Growth of World Population.* Washington, D.C.: National Academy of Sciences, 1963.

Ness, Gayl. "The Measurement and Meaning of Economic Growth." In *The Sociology of Economic Development,* edited by Gayl Ness, pp. 3-15. New York: Harper & Row, 1970.

Notestein, Frank W., and Regine K. Stix. *Controlled Fertility.* Baltimore: Williams and Wilkins, 1940.

Oechsli, Frank, and Arjun Adlakha. "Temporal and Regional Variation in Brazilian Natality, 1940-1970." Unpublished paper, Food Research Institute, Stanford University, Stanford, California, 1974.

_____, and B. Edmonston. "Natality Decline and Social-Economic Change in Venezuela." Unpublished paper, Food Research Institute, Stanford University, Stanford, California, 1974.

_____, and Dudley Kirk. "Modernization and the Demographic Transition in Latin America and the Caribbean." Report to the National Institute of Child Health and Human Development for Contract NICHD-70-2189, 1974. (Also Forthcoming in *Economic Development and Cultural Change,* January 1975.)

Office Permanent de l'Institut International de Statistique. *Annuaire International de Statistique.* The Hague: W.P. Van Stockum and Sons, 1916.

Ogburn, William F. *Social Change.* New York: The Viking Press, 1922.

_____, and Meyer F. Nimkoff. *Technology and the Changing Family.* Boston: Houghton Mifflin, 1955.

Ohlin, Goran. *Population Control and Economic Development.* Paris: Development Centre of the Organisation for Economic Co-operation and Development, 1967.

Parsons, Talcott. *Societies: Evolutionary and Comparative Perspectives.* Englewood Cliffs, N.J.: Prentice-Hall, Inc., 1966.

Petersen, William. "The Demographic Transition in the Netherlands." *American Sociological Review,* 25:334-47, 1960.

_____. *Population.* 2nd ed. London: Macmillan Co., 1969.

_____. "The Malthus-Godwin Debate, Then and Now." *Demography,* 8:13-26, 1971.

Pool, D.I. "Ghana: The Attitudes of Urban Males toward Family Size and Family Limitation." *Studies in Family Planning,* 60:12-17, 1970.

Population Council. "Roman Catholic Fertility and Family Planning." *Studies in Family Planning,* 34:1-24, 1968.

_____. "World Population: Status Report, 1974." *Reports on Population Family Planning,* No. 15, 1974.

Potter, G., Jr., and P.C. Sagi. *The Third Child.* Princeton: Princeton University Press, 1967.

Requena, Mariano B. "The Problem of Induced Abortion in Latin America." *Demography,* 5:785-99, 1968.

Ridley, Jeanne Clare, M.C. Sheps, J.W. Linger, and J.A. Menken. "The Effects of Changing Mortality on Natality: Some Estimates from a Simulation Model." *Milbank Memorial Fund Quarterly,* 45:77-97, 1967.

Roberts, George W. *The Population of Jamaica.* Cambridge, Eng.: University Press, 1957.

Robinson, W.C. "The Development of Modern Population Theory." *American Journal of Economics and Sociology,* 23:375-92, 1964.

_____. "Ecological Correlations and the Behavior of Individuals." *American Sociological Review,* 15:351-57, 1950.

Rothman, Ana M. "Evolution of Fertility in Argentina and Uruguay." Demography Department of the Center for Social Research of the Torcuato Di Tella Institute, Buenos Aires, Argentina, 1969. (Mimeographed.)

Ryder, Norman B. "On Sociological Determinants of Fertility in the United States." Paper presented at the International Symposium on Statistical Problems in Population Research, Honolulu, Hawaii, August 2-6, 1971.

_____, and C.F. Westoff. *Reproduction in the United States, 1965.* Princeton: Princeton University Press, 1971.

Silver, Morris. "Births, Marriages and Business Cycle in the United States." *Journal of Political Economy,* 74:237-55, 1965.

Sjoberg, Gideon. *The Pre-Industrial City, Past and Present.* Glencoe: The Free Press, 1960.

Slicher van Bath, Bernard H. "Historical Demography and the Social and Economic Development of the Netherlands." *Daedalus,* 97:604-21, 1968.

Spengler, Joseph J. *France Faces Depopulation.* Durham, N.C.: Duke University Press, 1938.

_____. "Demographic Factors and Early Modern Economic Development." *Daedalus,* 97:433-46, 1968.

Stinner, William F. "Modernization, Nuptiality, and Fertility in Latin America." Unpublished doctoral dissertation, Pennsylvania State University, 1968.

Stolnitz, George J. "The Demographic Transition." *Population: The Vital Revolution.* Edited by Ronald Freedman. New York: Doubleday, 1964, pp. 30-46.

Stycos, J. Mayone. *Human Fertility in Latin America: Sociological Perspectives.* Ithaca, N.Y.: Cornell University Press, 1968.

_____. *Ideology, Faith, and Family Planning in Latin America.* New York: McGraw-Hill Book Company, Inc., 1971.

Sundbarg, Gustav. *Aperçus Statistiques Internationaux.* Demographic Monographs, Vol. 14. Edited by M. Perlman. New York: Gorden and Breach, 1908.

Tabbarah, Riad B. "Toward a Theory of Demographic Development." *Economic Development and Cultural Change*, 19:257-76, 1971.

Taeuber, Irene B. "Japan's Demographic Transition Re-Examined." *Population Studies*, 14:28-39, 1960.

Tanner, J.M. "The Trend towards Earlier Physical Maturation." Pp. 40-65 in *Biological Aspects of Social Problems.* Edited by J.E. Meade and A.S. Parkes. London: Oliver and Boyd, 1965.

Thomas, Dorothy S. *Social and Economic Aspects of Swedish Population Movements, 1750-1933.* New York: Macmillan, 1941.

Thompson, Warren S. "Population." *American Journal of Sociology*, 34:959-75, 1929.

_____. *Population and Peace in the Pacific.* Chicago: University of Chicago Press, 1945.

Tsubouchi, Yoshiro. "Changes in Fertility in Japan by Region: 1920-1965." *Demography*, 7:121-34, 1970.

UNESCO (United Nations Educational, Scientific, and Cultural Organization). *Statistical Yearbook*, 1967-1969. Louvain, Belgium: UNESCO, 1968-1970.

United Nations. *Demographic Yearbook.* Various editions. New York: United Nations, 1949-70.

_____. *Statistical Yearbook.* Various editions. New York: United Nations, 1949-70.

_____. Department of Economic and Social Affairs. "Methods for Population Projections by Sex and Age." *Manual III, Manuals on Methods of Estimating Population* (ST/SOA/Series A, Population Studies, Number 25). New York: United Nations, 1956.

_____. *Population Bulletin Number 7.* New York: United Nations, 1963.

_____. *Estimates of Crude Birth Rates, Crude Death Rates, and Expectations of Life at Birth, Regions and Countries, 1950-1965.* New York: United Nations, 1969.

_____. *Urban and Rural Population: Individual Countries 1950-1985 and Major Areas 1950-2000.* New York: United Nations, 1970.

_____. *Population and Vital Statistics Report—Data as of 1 January, 1974.* Series A, Volume XXVI, No. 1. New York: United Nations, 1974.

Van de Walle, Etienne. "Marriage and Marital Fertility." *Daedalus*, 97:486-501, 1968.

_____, and John Knodel. "Demographic Transition and Fertility Decline: The European Case.." Pp. 47-55 in *Contributed Papers of the Sydney*

Conference of the International Union for the Scientific Study of Population. Canberra: Australian National University Press, 1967.

Vasquez, J.L. "Fertility Decline in Puerto Rico." *Demography*, 5:855-65, 1968.

Vries, Egbert de, and José Medina Echavarria. *Social Aspects of Economic Development in Latin America.* Vol. I. Paris: UNESCO, 1963.

Weintraub, Robert. "The Birth Rate and Economic Development: An Empirical Study." *Econometrica*, 40:812-17, 1962.

Weller, Robert H., and Donald Sly. "Modernization and Demographic Change: A World View." *Rural Sociology*, 34, 1969.

Westoff, Charles F., and R.H. Potvin. *College Women and Fertility Values.* Princeton: Princeton University Press, 1967.

Wonnacott, Ronald J., and Thomas H. Wonnacott. *Econometrics.* New York: John Wiley & Sons, Inc., 1970.

Wrigley, E.A. "Mortality in Pre-Industrial England: The Example of Colyton, Devon, over Three Centuries." *Daedalus*, 97:546-80, 1968.

Wyon, John B., and John E. Gordon. *The Khanna Study.* Cambridge, Mass.: Harvard University Press, 1971.

Yaukey, David. *Fertility Differences in a Modernizing Country.* Princeton: Princeton University Press, 1961.

Young, Ruth C. "The Plantation Economy and Industrial Development in Latin America" and "Economic Development in Latin America." *Economic Development and Cultural Change*, 18:342-61, 1970.

Yule, G.U. "Changes in Marriage and Birth Rates in England and Wales during the Past Half-Century." *Journal of the Royal Statistical Society*, 69:100-32, 1906.

Index

Index

abortion, 25, 28, 50, 119
acceleration of change, xxi, 85, 89, 95, 101, 105, 148, 152. *See also* type of change
Adlahka, Arjun, 114, 159
African cultural-racial group, 57, 117, 119
age-sex standardized birth rate, 67, 72, 124
age structure, 72, 76, 124, 152
aggregation bias, 61-62
Albania, 3
Amerindian, 36, 57, 117, 118, 119, 149
arable land, 77
Argentina, 51, 83, 86, 89, 101, 107
Arriaga, Eduardo, 38, 46, 74
Asia, 29. *See also* particular countries
autocorrelation, 69-70, 123, 140-143, 150

Banks, Arthur S., 75, 104, 109, 113
"benchmark" levels, 78, 94, 100. *See also* specific indicator
Blake, Judith, 44
Bohrnstedt, George, 66
Brazil, 51, 111, 114, 148, 160
Bulgaria, 26
business cycles, 48-49, 132, 146. *See also* economic expansion and resources, family

Carlsson, Gösta, 22, 26, 48
Catholicism, 17, 51-52, 149
causal model, 54
CELADE, 73
census data, 1970, 114
change, rates of, 78
Chile, 81, 83, 86, 89, 107
class (social), 2, 4, 6, 43
Collver, O. Andrew, 72-73, 74, 107
communication, 31
consensual unions, 36, 37, 53
contraception, 6, 50-52. *See also* family planning programs
Costa Rica, 73, 110, 132
cross-lag coefficients, 123, 138-139, 150

crude birth rate, 72
crude death rate, 74, 140
Cuba, 83, 86, 89, 107
cultural background. *See* culture
cultural lag, 44
culture, xx, 29, 30, 36, 37, 49-50, 53, 57-58, 60, 65-66, 72, 77-78, 116-120, 144, 149

Davis, Kingsley, 44, 75
Demeny, Paul, 18
demographic transition, in developing nations, 27-33; in Europe, 15-24; in Japan, 25-27; theory of the, 1-14, 41, 120
density, population, 32. *See also* land availability
Depression, 2, 84
desired family size, 9, 42
development. *See* socioeconomic development
diffusion, 22, 38, 62-63
Durbin, J., 141

Easterlin, Richard, 48
East-Indian cultural-racial group, 117, 119
ecological fallacy, 61-62
economic expansion, 68, 72, 77, 131-132, 137, 146, 150. *See also* business cycles
Edmonston, Barry, 114, 158
education, 6, 20, 29, 30, 36, 37, 101, 102, 104, 107, 125, 150. *See also* literacy; school enrollment
El Salvador, 81, 110
England, 19-20, 21, 86
errors, correlation of, 69-70, 140-141. *See also* autocorrelation
Europe, demographic transition in, 15-24
expectation of life, 74, 129-130, 139, 140
expectations, 60, 77

family planning programs, 50, 51-52
family structure, 52-53, 119. *See also* kinship; sex roles

175

fecundity, 17, 37, 45
"floor" effect, 28
France, 6, 17, 18, 19-20, 83, 85
Freedman, Ronald, 7
Friedlander, Dov, 21

Galton, Francis, 62-63
Germany, 19, 85, 93
Godwin, William, 2
Goldscheider, Calvin, xix
Goode, William, 36-38
Goubert, Pierre, 18
gross reproduction rates, 90
Guatemala, 83, 110
Guyana, 83, 110, 111

Hanley, Susan, 25
Heer, David, 31, 34, 36, 37-38
Hofstee, E., 17
Hungary, 18

illegitimacy, 53, 119, 149
income, 31, 48, 61-62, 76, 91, 138.
  See also national product
income distribution, 76
infant mortality. See mortality, infant
infanticide, 26
"infrastructure", 29
Indian. See Amerindian
inheritance, 8, 17, 47, 49
"insurance" births, 8, 46
intermediate variables, 44
Ireland, 18, 85
Islam, 29
Italy, 55, 84, 86, 90

Jamaica, 101, 110, 111
James, Preston, 77
Janowitz, Barbara, 29, 32, 127
Japan, 25-27

kinship, 4, 7, 37, 42, 43, 52-53, 119
Kirk, Dudley, 29, 30, 48
Kuhn, Thomas, 11

lag times, xx, 20, 22, 24, 43, 70-71,
  97, 121, 123, 134-138, 150
land availability, xxi, 16, 21, 25, 32,
  47, 48-49, 59, 67, 68, 72, 76-77,
  130-131, 132-133, 145, 150
land supply. See land availability

land tenure, 47, 49
Latin America, 28, 33-40, 61
linearity, 66, 121, 123, 133-134, 151
literacy, 37, 75, 111. See also education; school enrollment
Livi Bacci, Massimo, 18, 19, 36, 90
Lorimer, Frank, 47

McGranahan, D., 33, 35
machismo, 119
Malthus, T., xx, 2-3, 5
marriage, 16, 36-37, 119
measurement error, 125, 134, 137,
  146, 150
measures, 71. See also measurement
  error
mestizo, 36, 37, 57, 118, 149
Mexico, 73, 111, 115, 132
Mill, John, 6
modernization. See socioeconomic
  development
mortality, xx, 7, 18, 20, 30, 38, 45-47,
  67, 71, 74, 93-97, 105, 110, 111,
  121, 128-130, 140, 145, 148; decline, 2, 5, 22, 27, 55, 56, 59, 64;
  effects on natality, 45-47; infant, 45,
  46, 73, 74, 129-130
multicollinearity, 68, 139-140
municipio, 111
Murumatsu, Minoru, 27

Naroll, Raoul, 63
natality, decline, xx, 2, 5-8, 22, 58,
  78, 81, 107, 110; decline rate, 23,
  27, 55, 64, 84-85, 87, 92, 148; effects of, 31, 67; increase, xx, 21, 36,
  37, 45, 146; measures, 71-73;
  periods of decline, 83-84; pre-transi-
  tion, 15, 24, 25, 145
national product, 29, 31, 39, 59, 67,
  76, 100, 101, 104, 125, 146, 150
Netherlands, 17, 19-20, 21
non-linear terms, 133-134, 151
Notestein, Frank, 6
nutrition, 45

Oechsli, Frank, 114
Ogburn, William, 44

Panama, 81, 90, 93, 101, 110
paradigm, 10, 12

Parsons, Talcott, 44
Population Council, 111
Portugal, 18-19, 55, 84, 86, 90
Puerto Rico, 90, 101, 110

race, 57, 77-78, 116, 117, 149
region, cultural. *See* culture
regional studies, 63
registration, births and deaths, 72
regression, 65-71, 73, 74, 75, 76,
   123-144
religion, 50-51 ; 149. *See also* Catholicism
religiosity, 51
residuals, 58, 60, 64, 118, 142-143;
   correlation of, 69-70, 140-143
resources, family, 48-49, 59, 68, 72,
   76-77, 130-133. *See also* economic
   expansion; land availability
reverse causation, 66, 138, 150
Ridley, Jeanne, 45
Roberts, George, 53
Rothman, Ana, 94, 107
Russia, 2, 26, 27, 55

school enrollment, 75-76, 101, 102,
   104, 125, 137, 150. *See also* education; literacy
secularism, 4, 18
separation, coefficient of, 65,
   107-108, 112
sex preference for children, 42
sex roles, 6, 7, 43, 52, 119, 149
significance tests, 69
simultaneous causation, 66. *See also*
   reverse causation

socioeconomic development, xx, 4-5,
   7, 22, 23, 27, 33, 35, 38, 44, 46, 48,
   55, 58, 64, 71, 74-76, 97-105, 120,
   124-128, 139, 146, 150
Spain, 18, 36, 55, 84, 86, 90, 93
Stinner, William, 37
Stix, Regine, 6
Stolnitz George, xix, 3, 6
Stycos, J. Mayone, 36-37, 53
survivorship, 46-47, 59, 74, 129-130.
   See also mortality; mortality, infant
Sweden, 21

Taeuber, Irene, 26
threshold, 56, 106, 121
Trinidad and Tobago, 101, 110
Tsubouchi, Yoshiro, 26

units of analysis, 41
urbanization, 4, 6, 21, 30, 36, 37, 68,
   75, 101, 102, 110, 111, 124, 125,
   136, 150
Uruguay, 83, 84, 86, 89, 94, 101, 107

values, 7; childbearing, 42, 139
Vasquez, J.L., 90
Venezuela, 111, 115, 148

weighting factors for family resources,
   68, 77, 132-133
West Indies, 53. *See also* specific
   nations
widowhood, 45
World Bank, 76, 101

About the Author

Steven E. Beaver is staff sociologist for the Seattle-Denver Income Maintenance Experiment and is primarily engaged in research on the effects of various income maintenance-negative tax programs on marital stability, family structure, and fertility. He is also directing two studies of socio-economic and demographic determinants of postwar American fertility trends through the Center for Policy Research. Professor Beaver received the B.A. from the University of Michigan in 1968, and the Ph.D. in sociology from Stanford University in 1972.

DATE DUE			